Belleville Ontario Book 2 in Colour Photos, Saving Our History One Photo at a Time

Photography
by Barbara Raué
2016

Series Name:
Cruising Ontario

Book 164: Belleville Book 2

Cover photo: 234 Ann Street, Page 17

Series Name: Cruising Ontario
The Authority on Saving Our History One Photo at a Time in colour photos

Books Available in Alphabetical Order:
Aberfoyle, Acton, Alton, Amherstburg, Ancaster, Arthur, Aylmer, Ayr, Bloomingdale, Brantford, Burlington, Caledon, Caledonia, Cambridge, Clifford, Conestogo, Delhi, Dorchester to Aylmer, Drayton, Drumbo, Dundas, Eden Mills, Elmira, Elora, Essex, Fergus, Guelph, Hagersville, Hamilton, Hanover, Harriston, Hespeler, Jarvis, Kingston, Kingsville, Kitchener, Linwood, Listowel, London, Lucknow, Mono, Mount Forest, Neustadt, New Hamburg, Niagara-on-the-Lake, Oakville, Orangeville, Orillia, Owen Sound, Palmerston, Peterborough, Petrolia, Port Elgin, Preston, Rockwood, Sarnia, Seaforth, Sheffield, Shelburne, Simcoe, Southampton, St. Jacobs, St. Marys, St. Thomas, Stoney Creek, Stratford, Thamesford, Tillsonburg, Waterdown, Waterford, Waterloo, Welland, Wellesley, Windsor, Wingham, Woodstock

Book 125-127: Woodstock
Book 128: Thamesford
Book 129-132: St. Marys
Book 133-136: Sarnia
Book 137: Petrolia
Book 138-139: Welland
Book 140-145: Kingston
Book 146-149: Ottawa
Book 150-151: Midland
Book 152: Penetanguishene
Book 153: Kemptville
Book 154: Cornwall
Book 155: Mariatown to Maitland

Book 156: Morrisburg
Book 157: Brockville
Book 158: Merrickville
Book 159: Smiths Falls
Book 160: Portland, Newboro
Book 161: Westport & Area
Book 162: Perth
Book 163-166: Belleville

Other Books by Barbara Raue

Coins of Gold

Arrows, Indians and Love

The Life and Times of Barbara
Volume 1: Inventions That Have Enhanced My Life
Volume 2: Entertainment That I Have Enjoyed
Volume 3: East Coast Trips
Volume 4: Olympics Have Always Intrigued Me
Volume 5: Wonders of the World
Volume 6: Caribbean Cruises We Have Enjoyed
Volume 7: Animals
Volume 8: Storms and Other Major Disasters in My Lifetime
Volume 9: Wars, Terrorist Attacks and Major Disasters

The Cromwell Family Book

Laura Secord Discovered

Daddy Where Are You?

Montana Series
Book 1: Montana Dream
Book 2: Life on the Montana Frontier
Book 3: Montana to Boston and Back
Book 4: Montana Sons Go to War

Visit Barbara's website to view all of her books
http://barbararaue.ca

Table of Contents

Belleville is a city located at the mouth of the Moira River on the Bay of Quinte in southeastern Ontario. It was the site of a Mississaugas' village in the eighteenth century. It was settled by United Empire Loyalists beginning in 1784. It was named Belleville in honor of Lady Arabella Gore in 1816, after a visit to the settlement by Sir Francis Gore and his wife.

It is known as the "friendly city" because it offers big city amenities along with small town friendliness, and a pleasing mixture of the historic and modern.

Belleville became an important railway junction with the completion of the Grand Trunk Railway in 1855. In 1858 the iron bridge over the Moira River at Bridge Street was constructed. Belleville's beautiful High Victorian Gothic city hall was built in 1872 to house the public market and administrative offices.

Due to its location near Lake Ontario, its climate is moderated by cooling hot summer days and warming cold days during the fall and winter.

Procter & Gamble, Kellogg's, Redpath, and Sears are corporations operating in Belleville. There are many other manufacturing sector companies which operate within the City of Belleville, including Sprague Foods, Sigma Stretch Film Canada, Reid's Dairy, and Parmalat Canada - Black Diamond Cheese Division, to name a few.

Belleville has an excellent yacht harbor, which is a picturesque stopping point for Great Lakes sailors and a favorite launch for sports fishing enthusiasts after walleye, pike and bass. Beautiful music chimes can be heard all year long from the City Hall clock tower, overlooking the new civic square and Farmers Market. Walking, biking and rollerblading can be enjoyed on the Bayshore and Riverfront Trails.

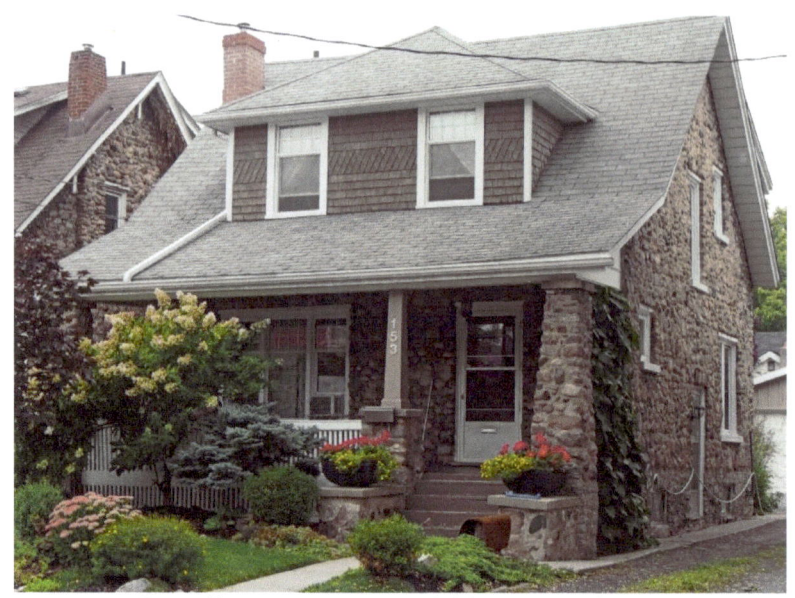

153 William Street – cobblestone, dormer

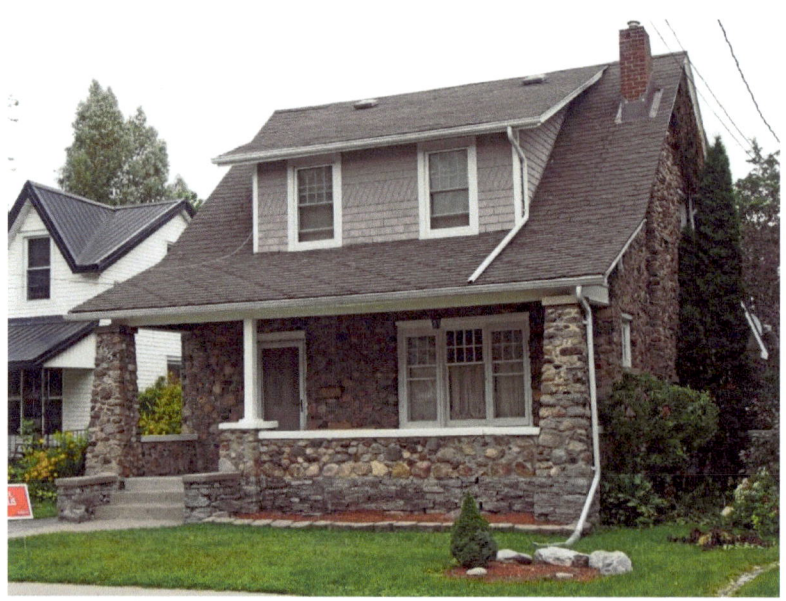

William Street – cobblestone, shed dormer

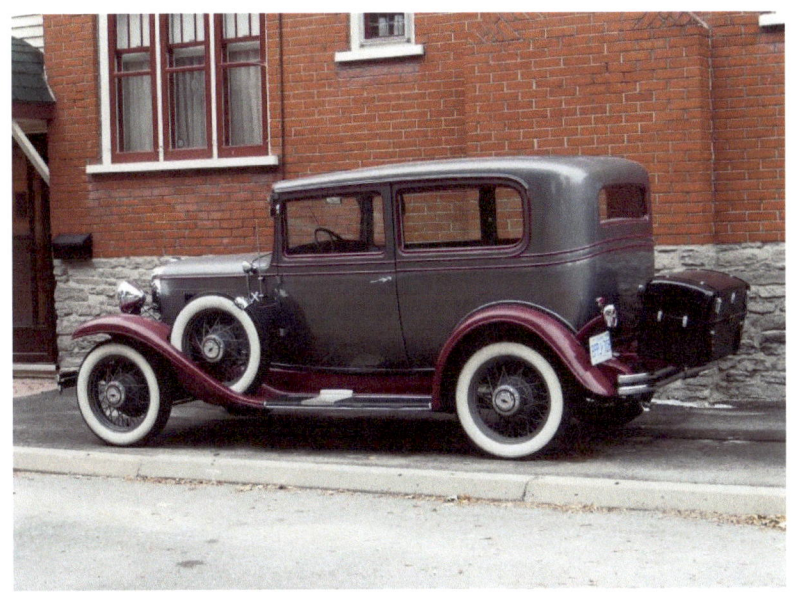

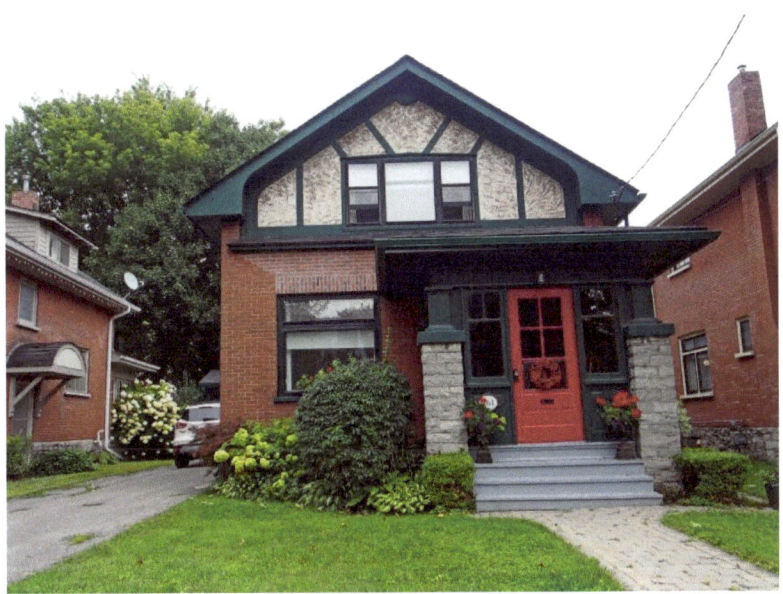

161 William Street – Tudor half-timbering in gable

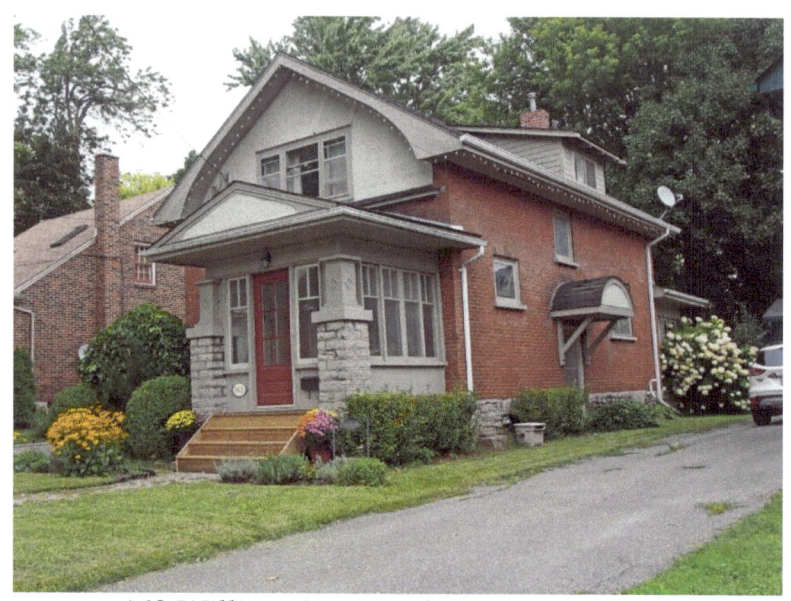

163 William Street – dormer, pediment

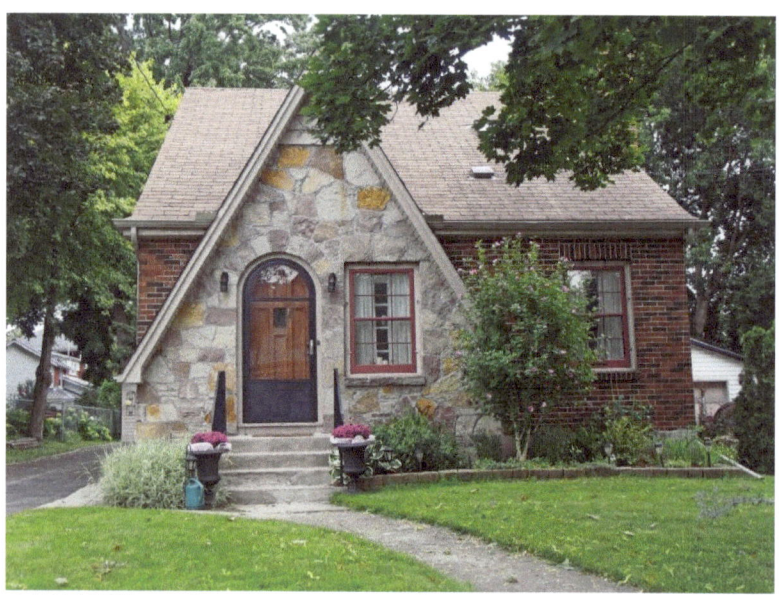

165 William Street – Arts and Crafts – stone and brick

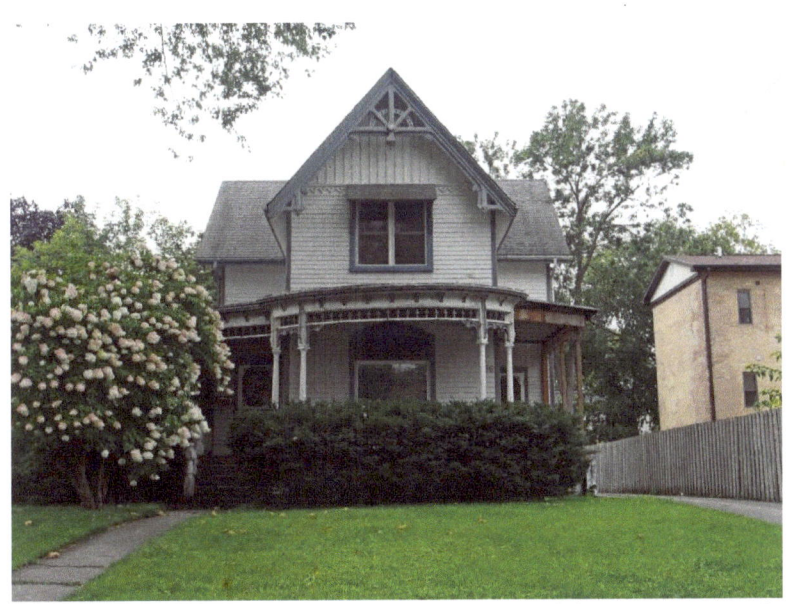

166 William Street – Gothic – trim on gable, ornate capital detailing on veranda support posts with spindle trim below cornice

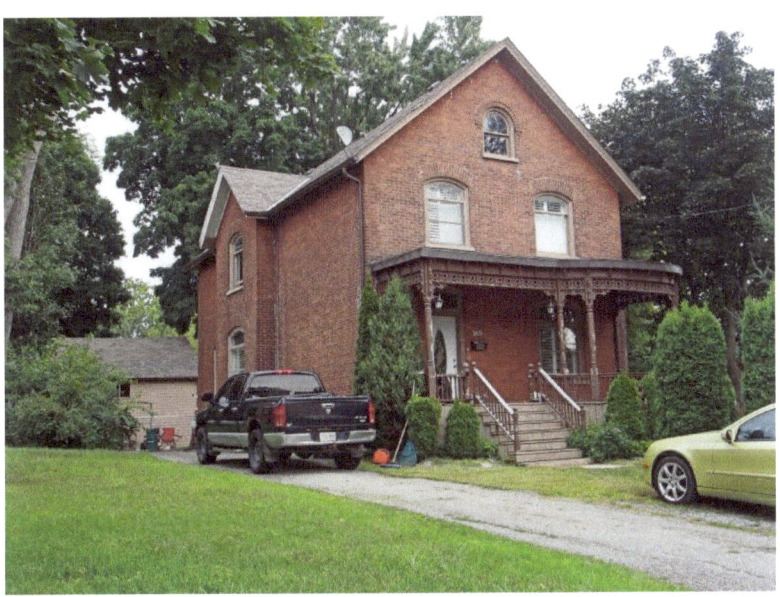

169 William Street - Gothic

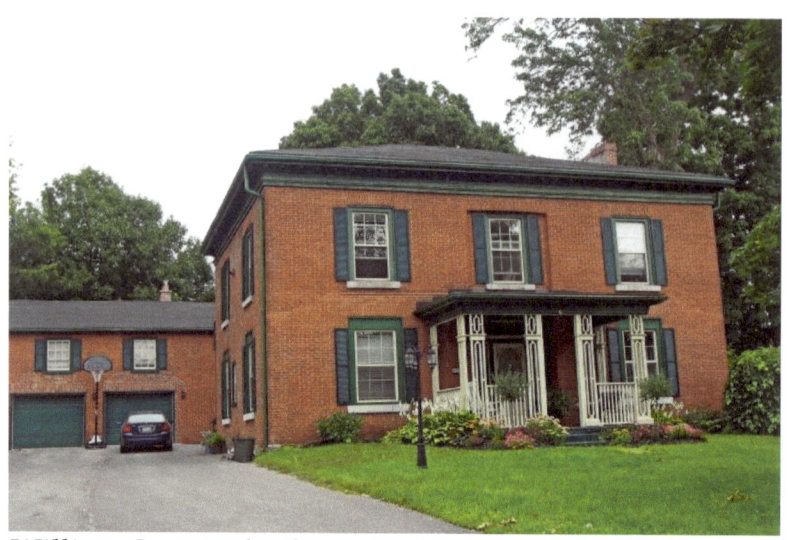

173 William Street – built 1851 – two-storey brick, hipped roof – heritage property

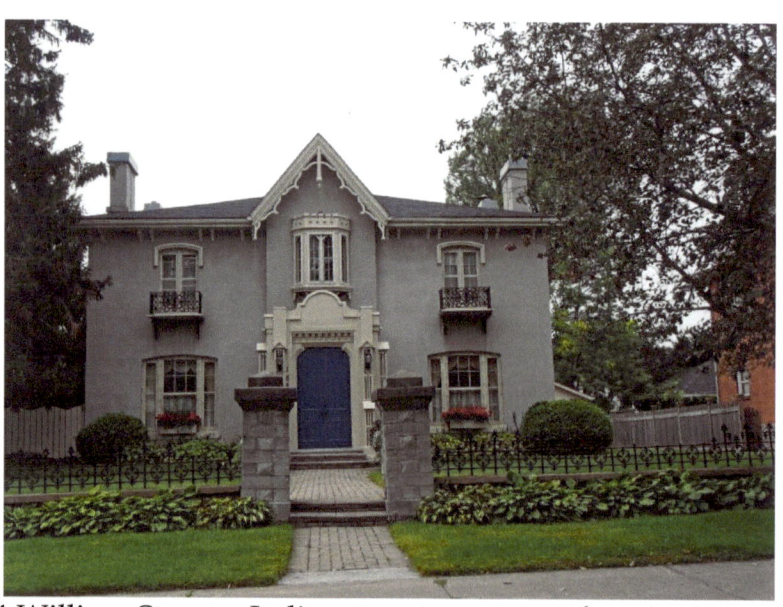

184 William Street – Italianate – two-storey frontispiece with verge board trim and finial on gable, cornice brackets, impressive entrance

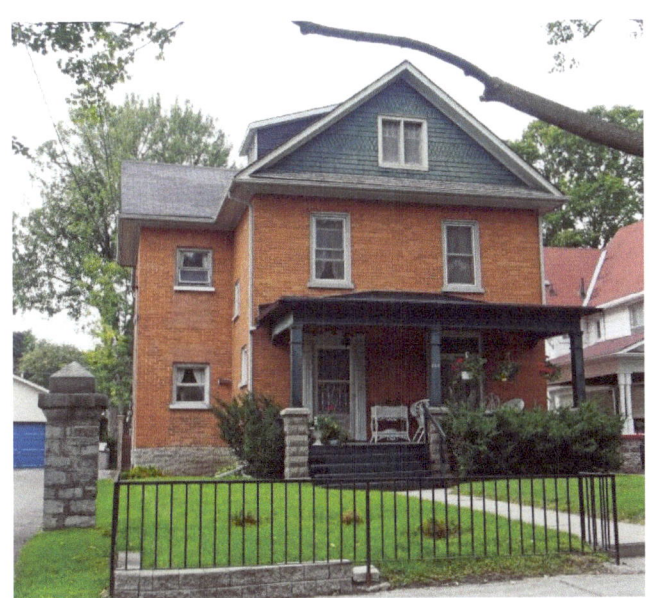

188 William Street - Edwardian

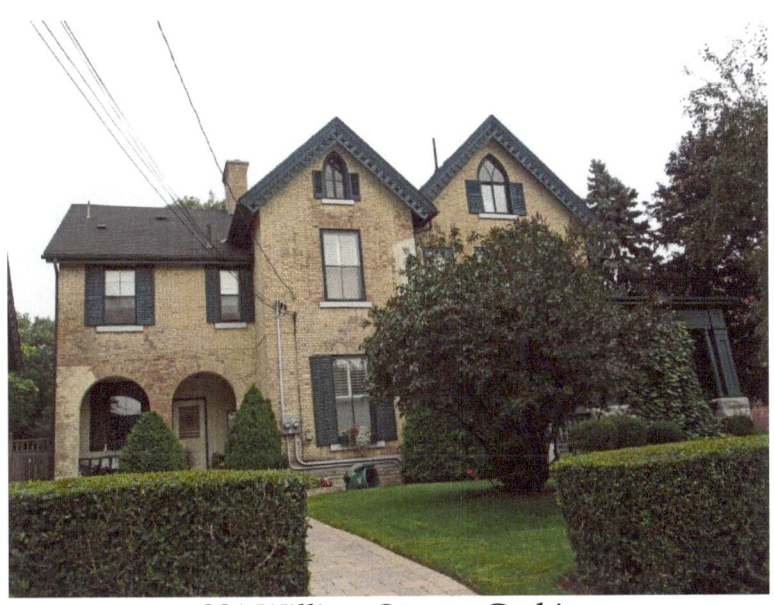

201 William Street - Gothic

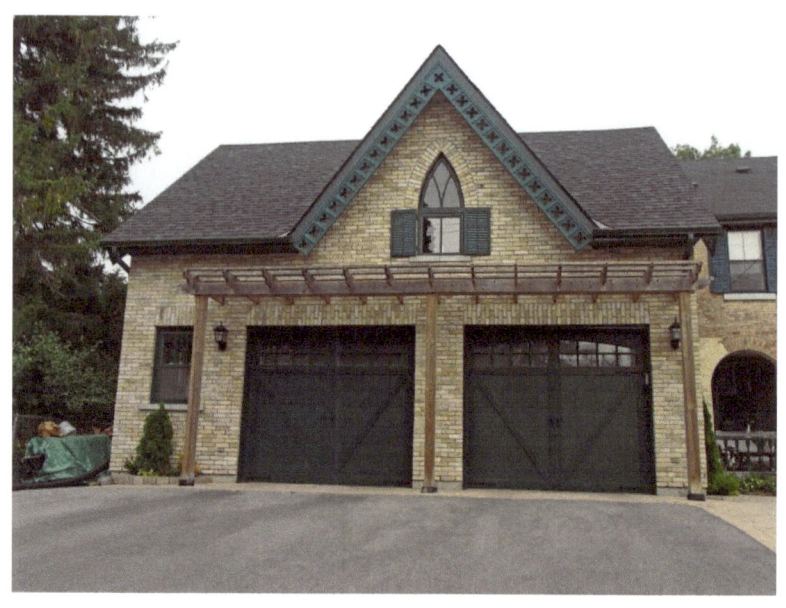

201 William Street – verge board trim on gables

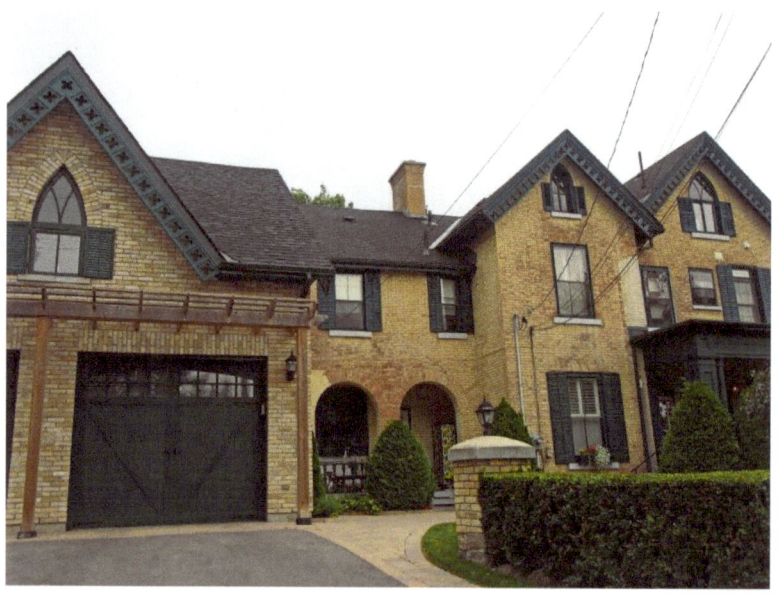

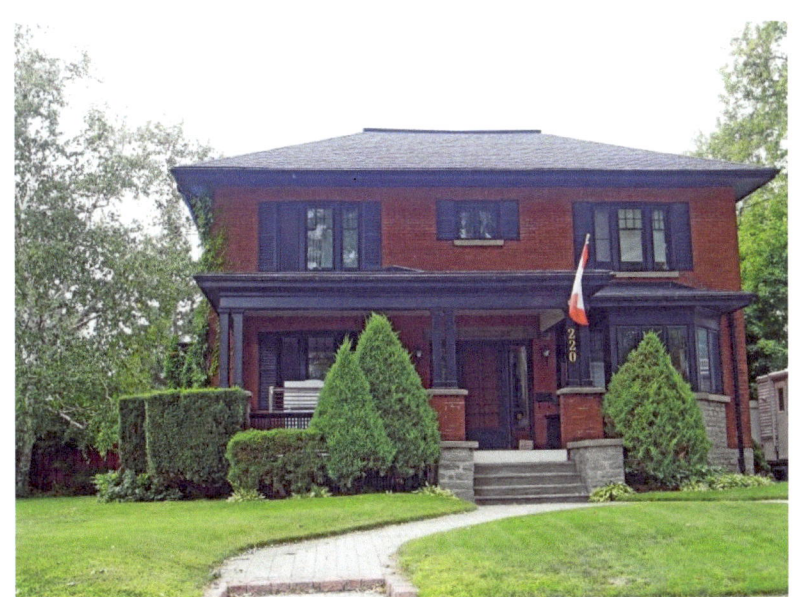

220 William Street – hipped roof

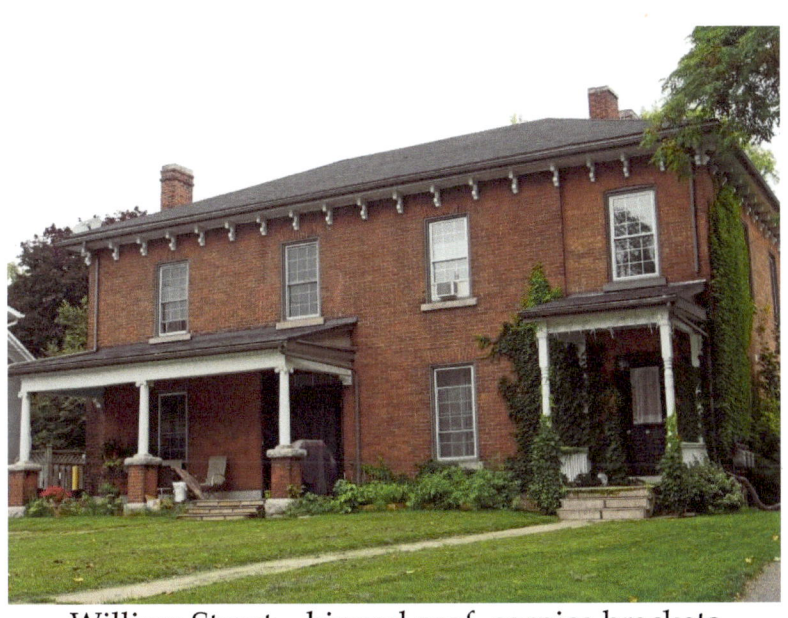

William Street – hipped roof, cornice brackets

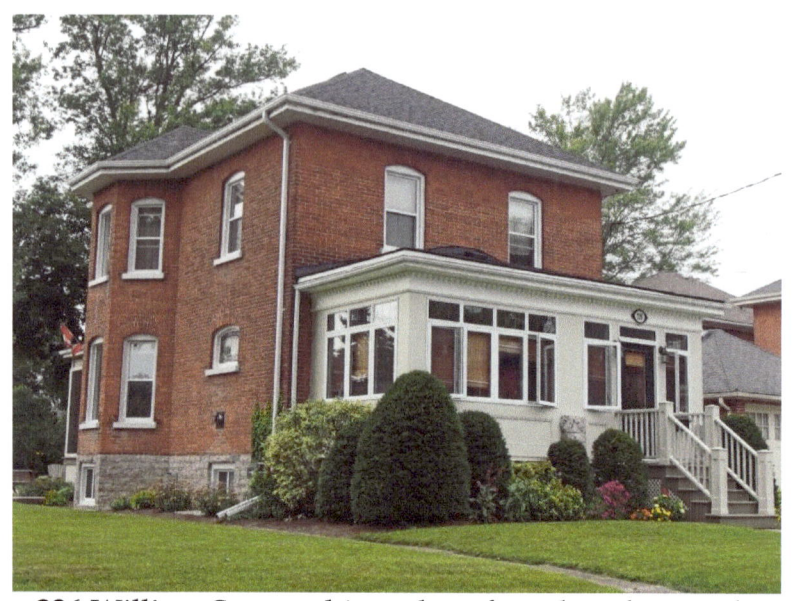

226 William Street – hipped roof, enclosed veranda

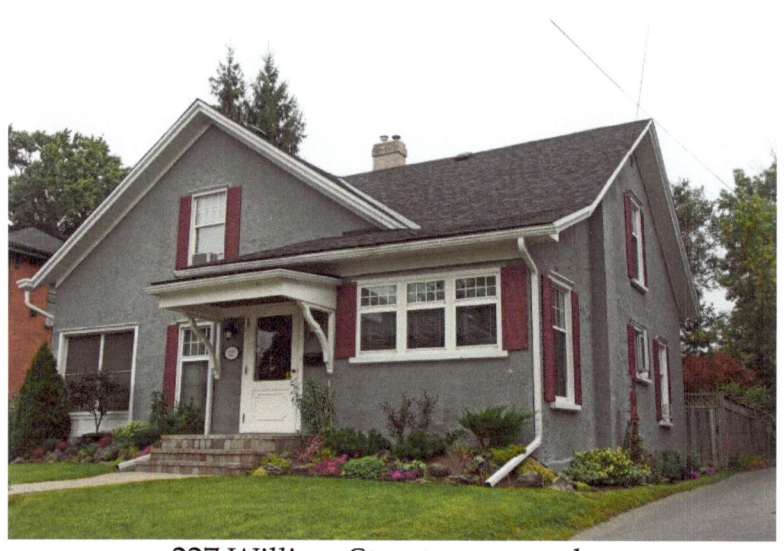

227 William Street - vernacular

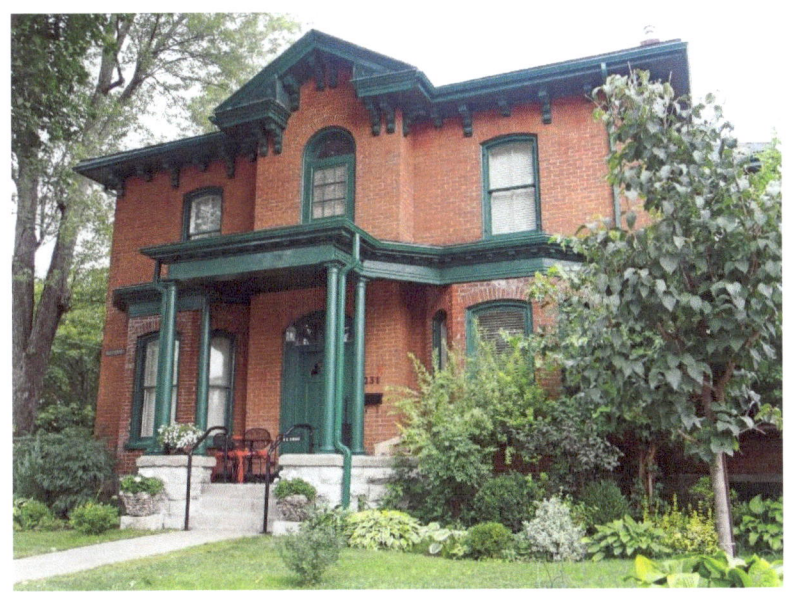

231 William Street – Italianate – two-storey frontispiece, cornice brackets

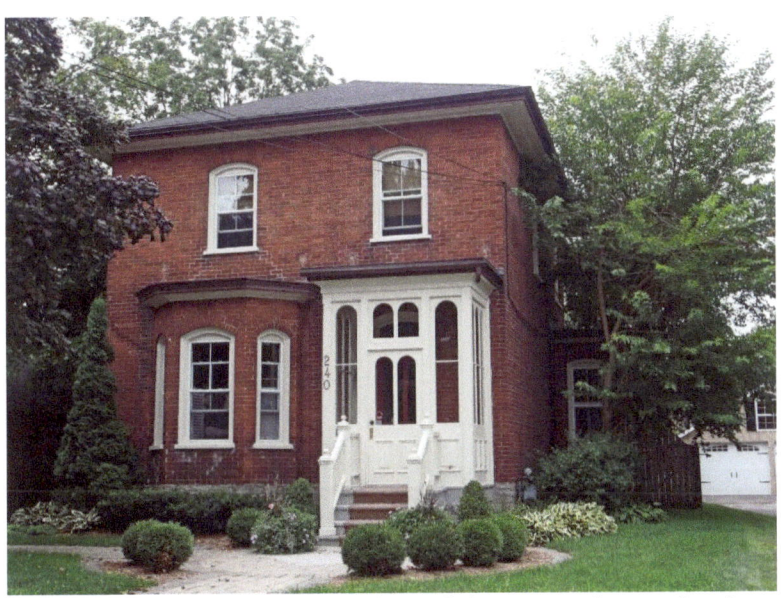

240 William Street – hipped roof, bay window – heritage property

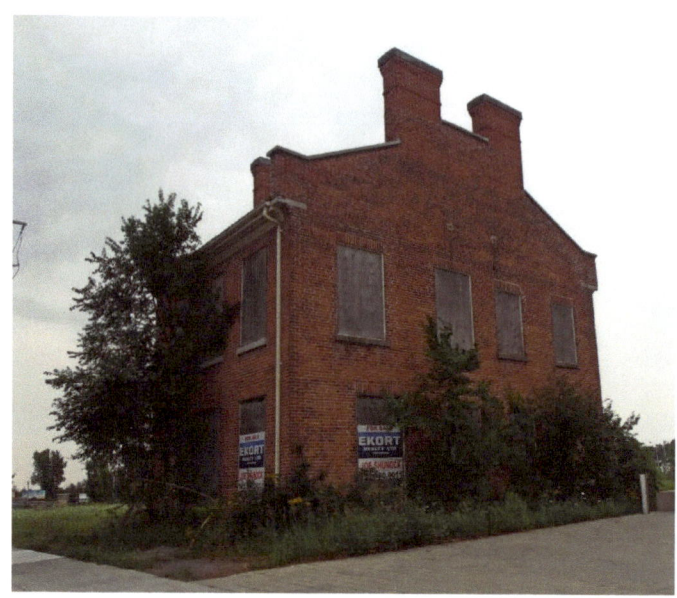

William Street

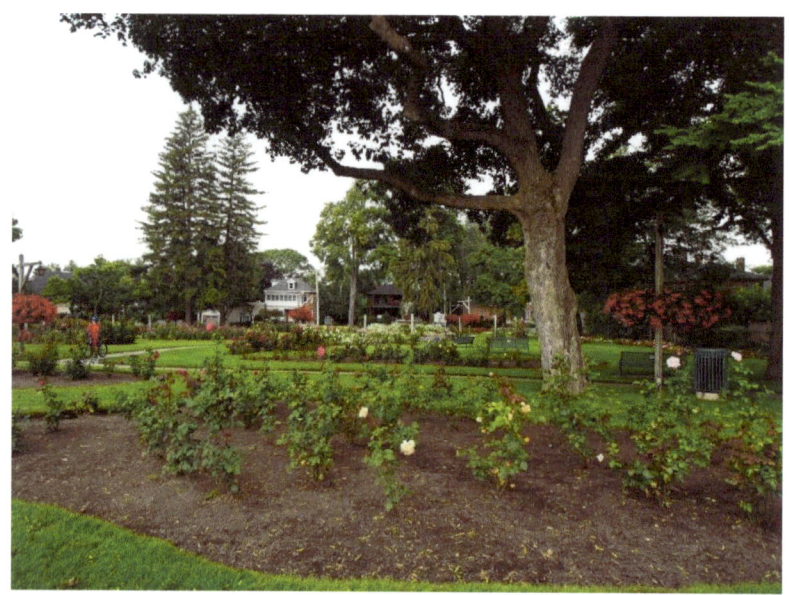

Corby Park – Rose Garden

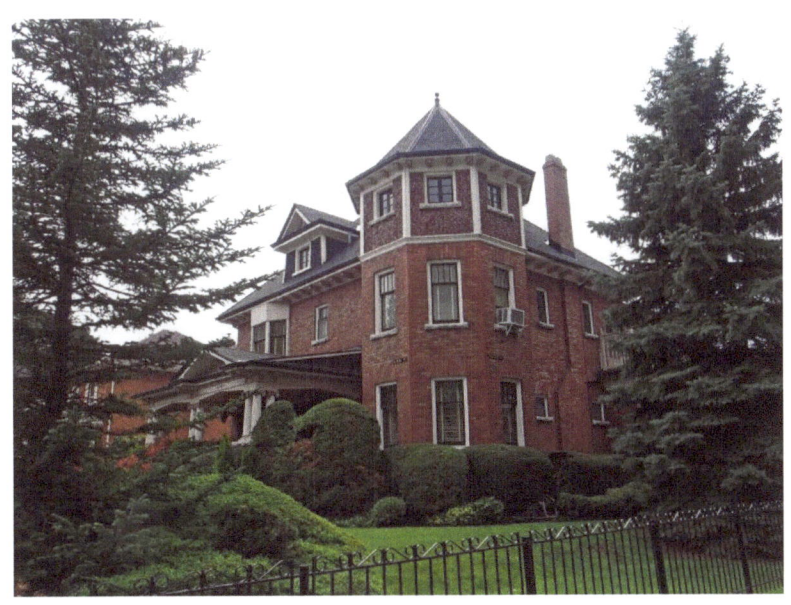

234 Ann Street (corner of Queen) – Ilcombe – Queen Anne style – three-storey tower, dormer, Ionic veranda pillars

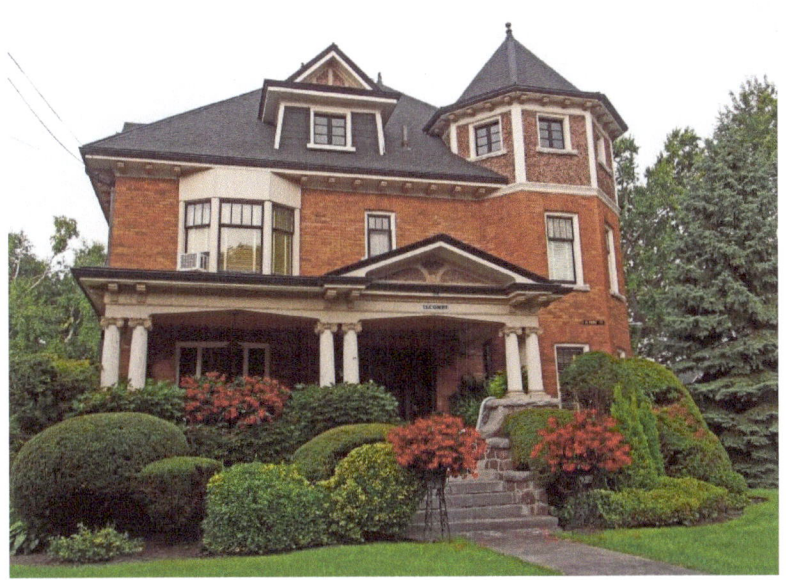

Oriel window, pediment

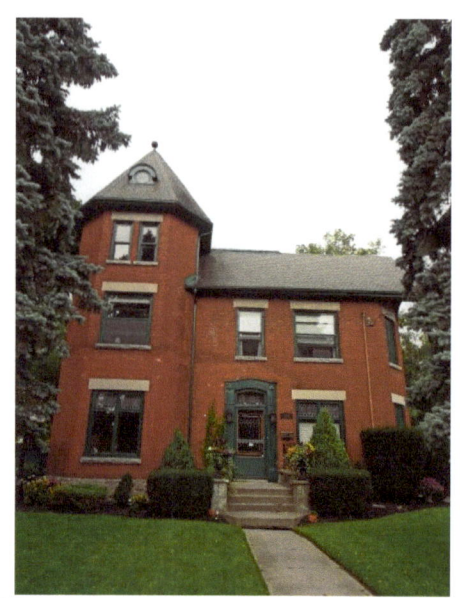

224 Ann Street – 3½-storey tower

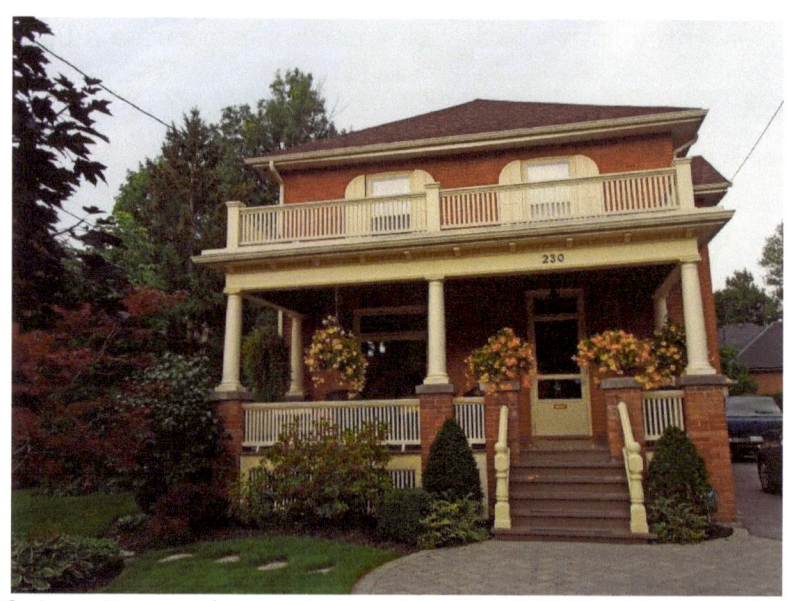

230 Ann Street – hipped roof, Doric veranda pillars on brick piers, second floor full-width balcony

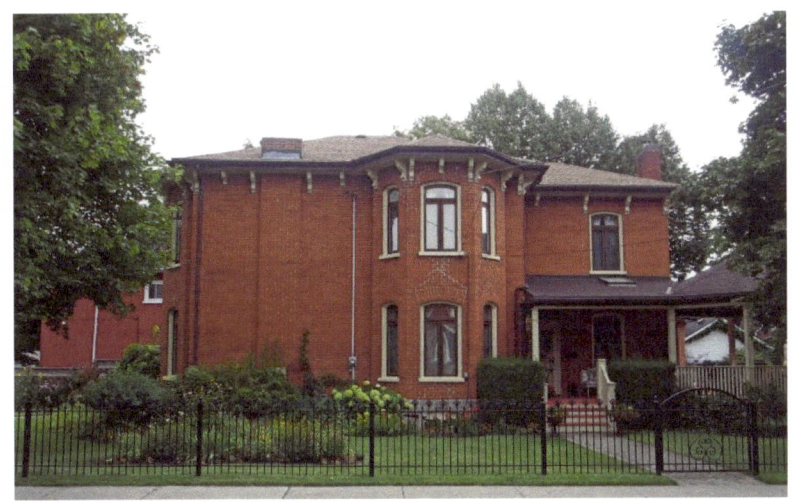

Ann Street – hipped roof, cornice brackets, two-storey tower-like bay

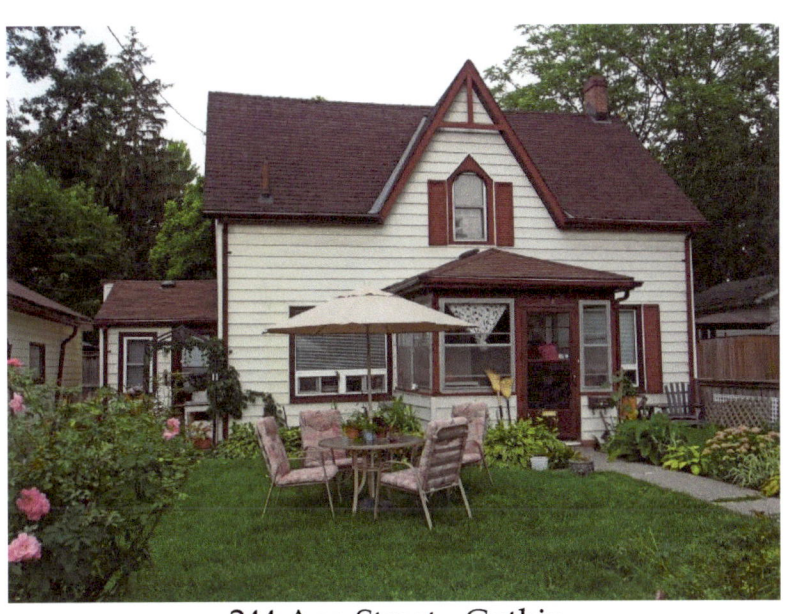

244 Ann Street - Gothic

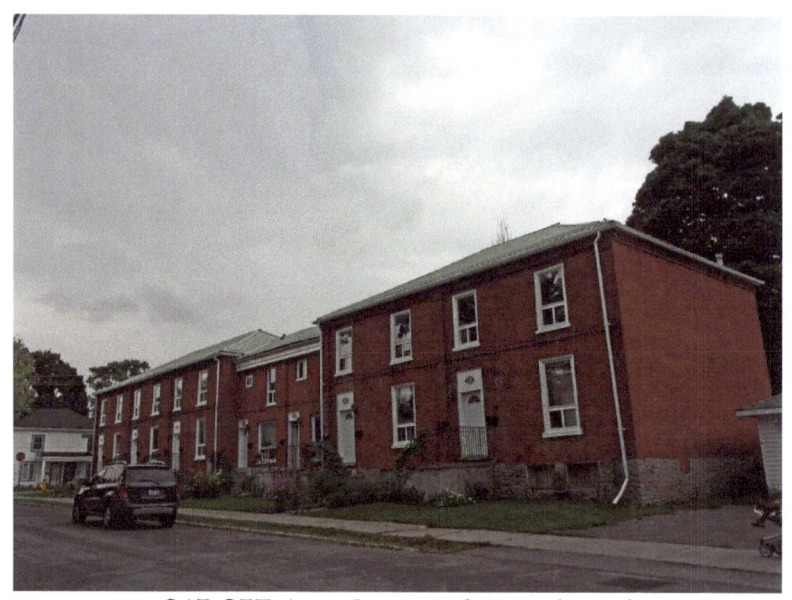

245-257 Ann Street – hipped roof

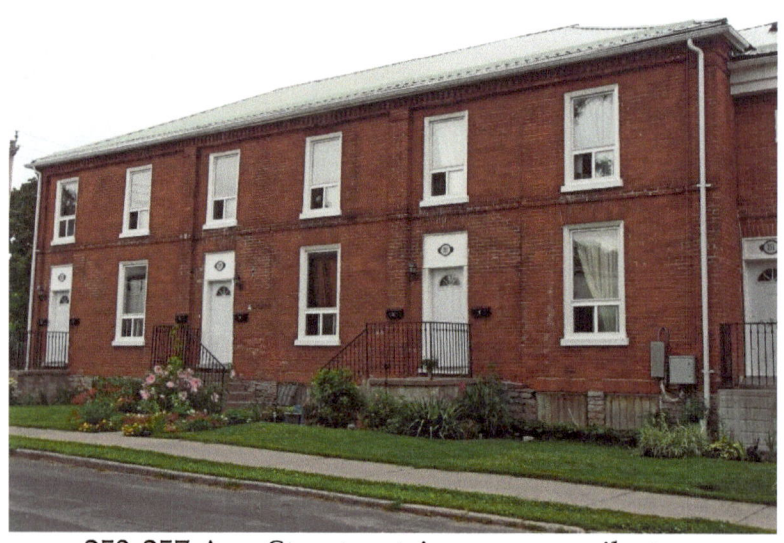

253-257 Ann Street – string course, pilasters

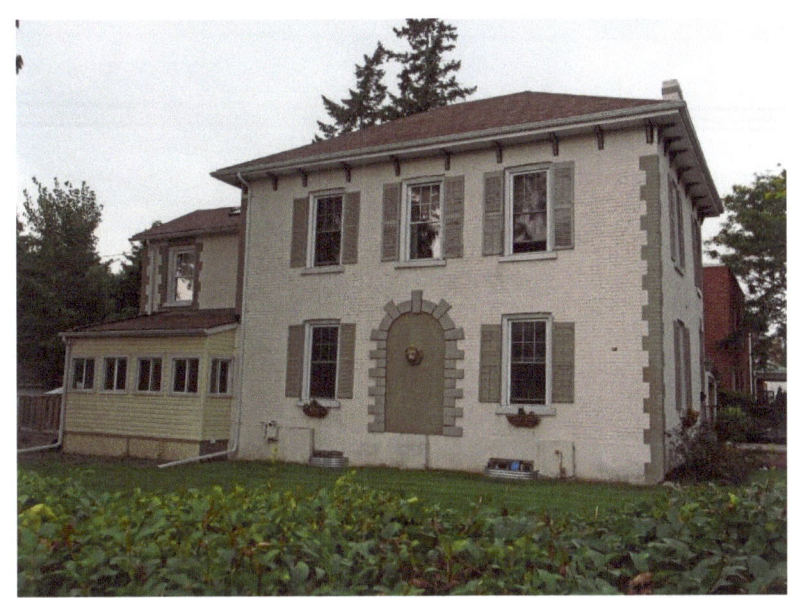

Ann Street – hipped roof, single cornice brackets, quoining

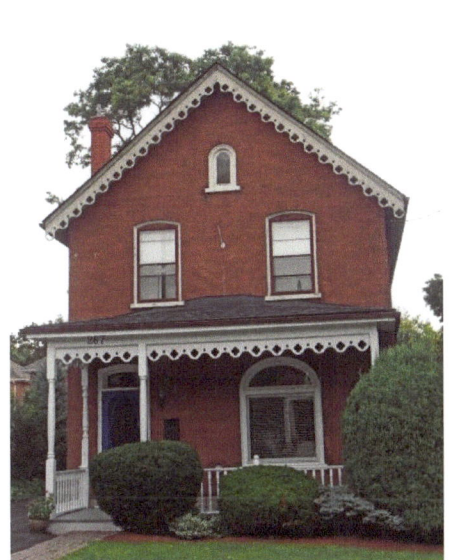

264 Ann Street
Gothic, verge board trim on
gable and veranda

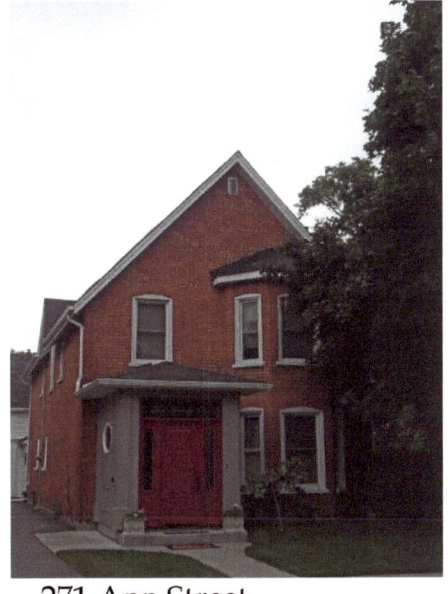

271 Ann Street
2-storey bay window

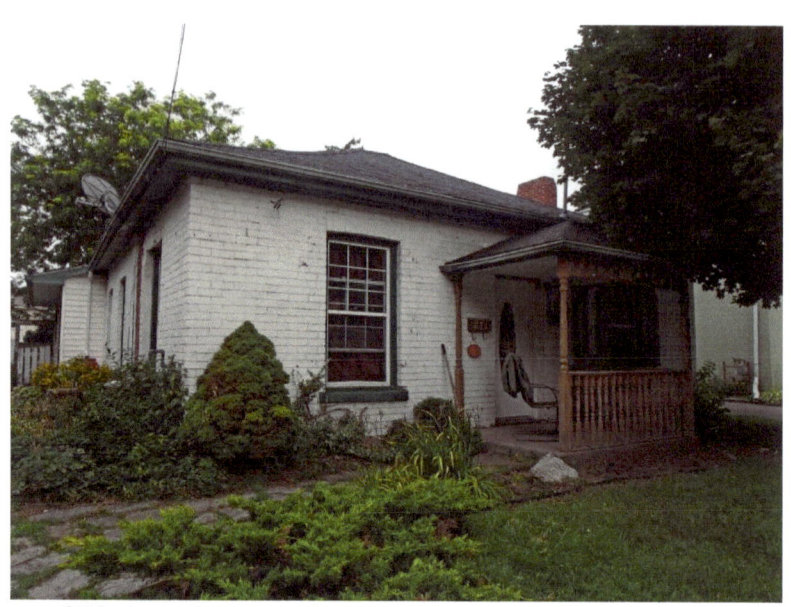

278 Ann Street – Ontario Cottage – hipped roof

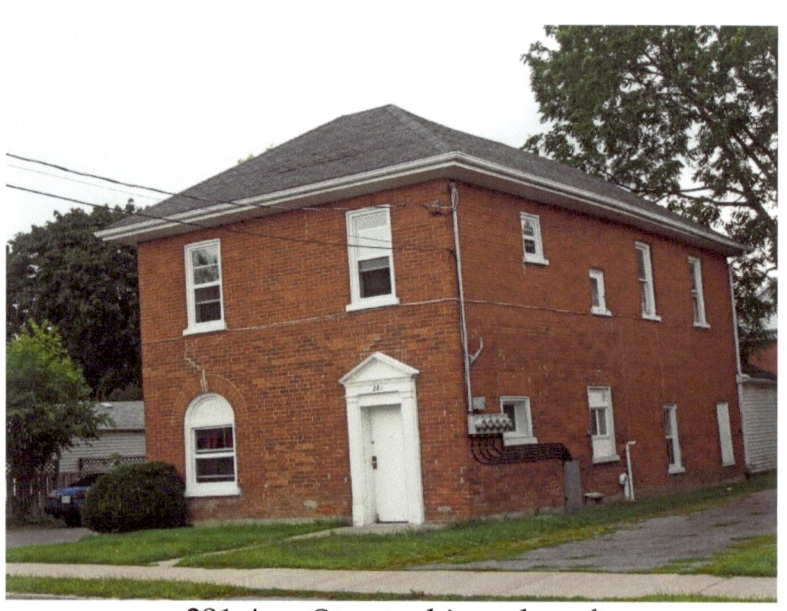

281 Ann Street – hipped roof

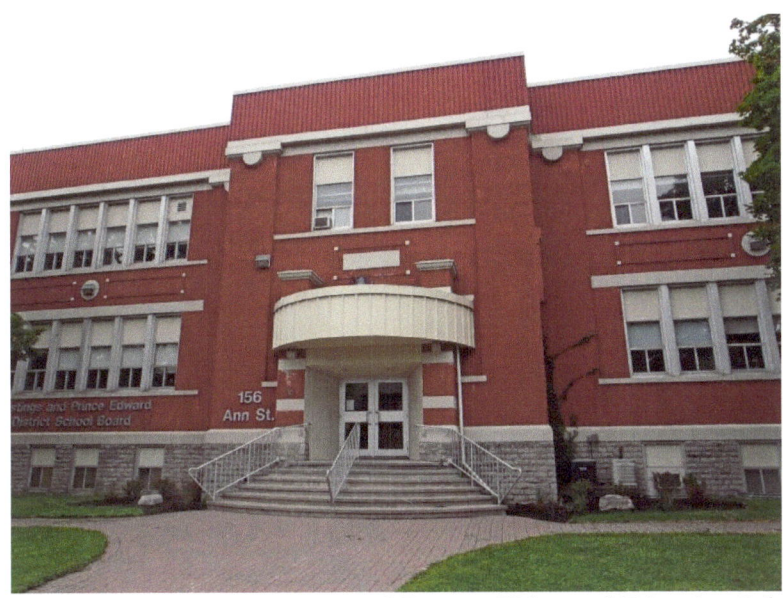

156 Ann Street – Hastings and Prince Edward District School Board

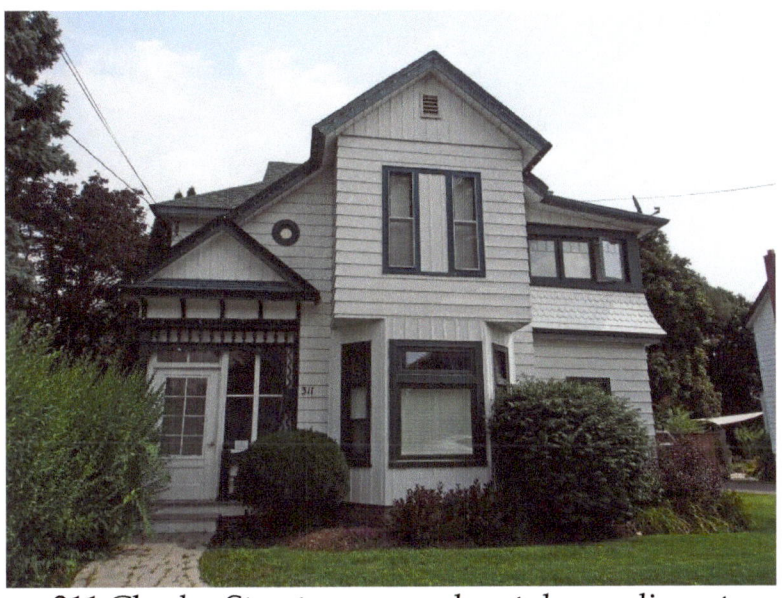

311 Charles Street – vernacular style - pediment

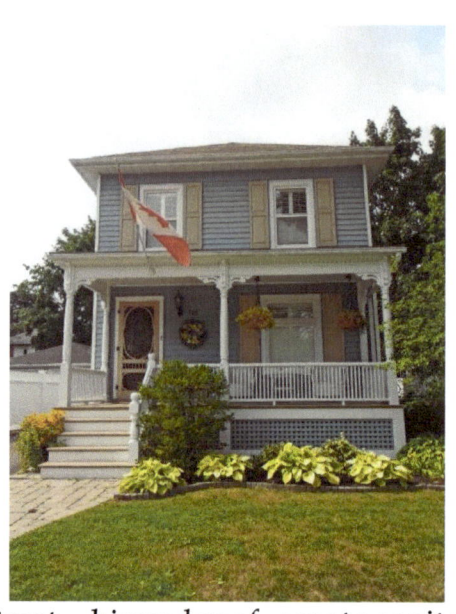

312 Charles Street – hipped roof, ornate capital detailing on veranda supports, open railing

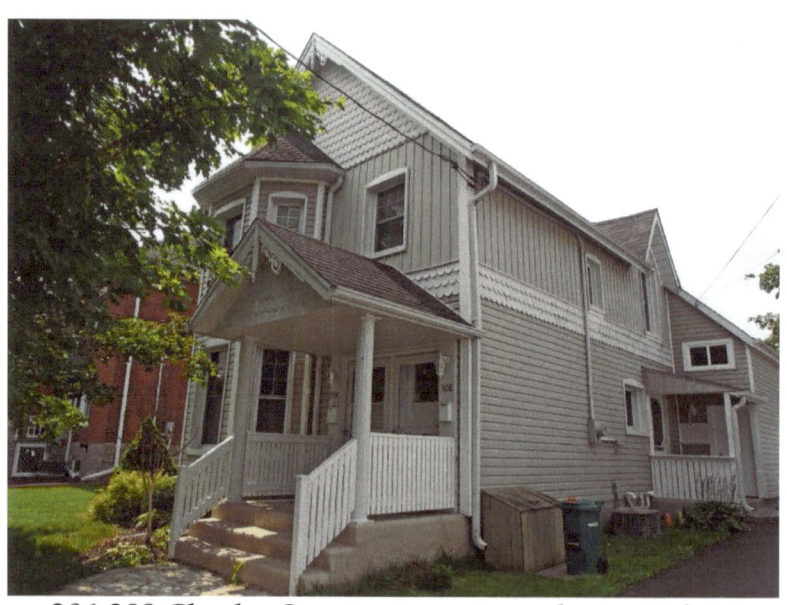

306-308 Charles Street – two-storey bay window

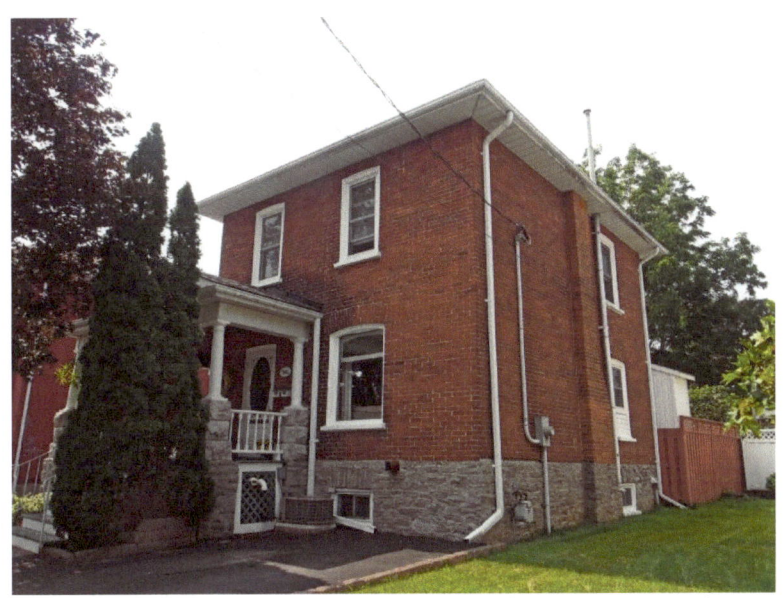

302 Charles Street – hipped roof, Doric capitals

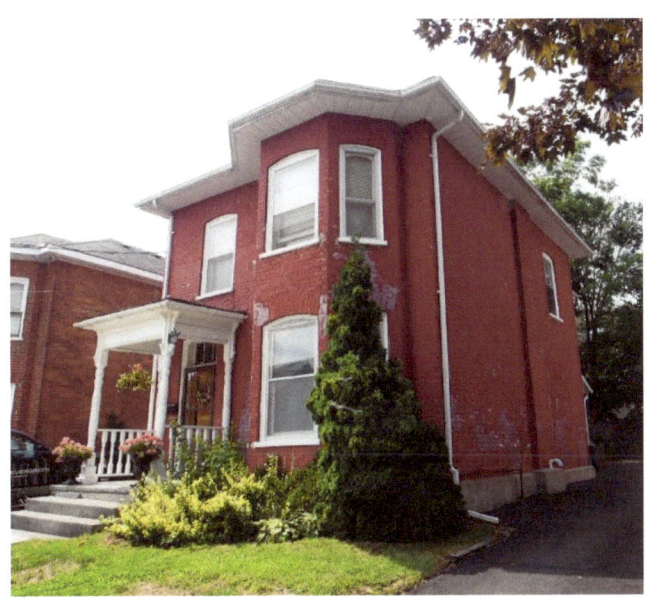

300 Charles Street – hipped roof, two-storey bay window,
turned wood porch supports

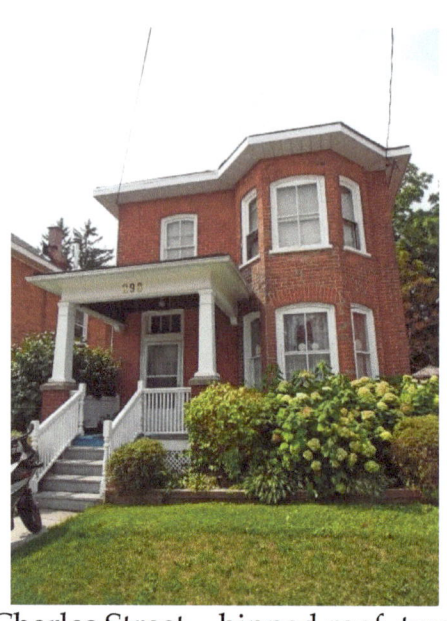

298 Charles Street – hipped roof, two-storey bay window

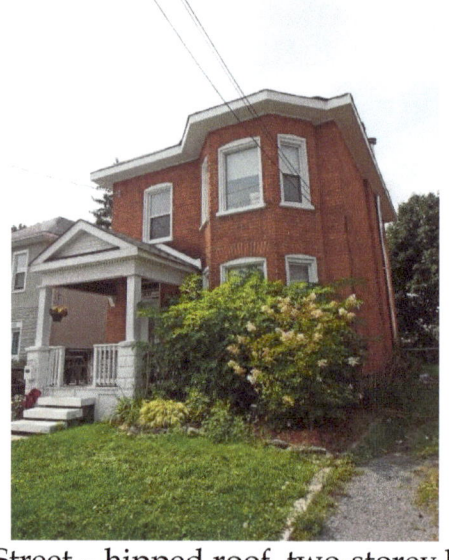

296 Charles Street – hipped roof, two-storey bay window, pediment

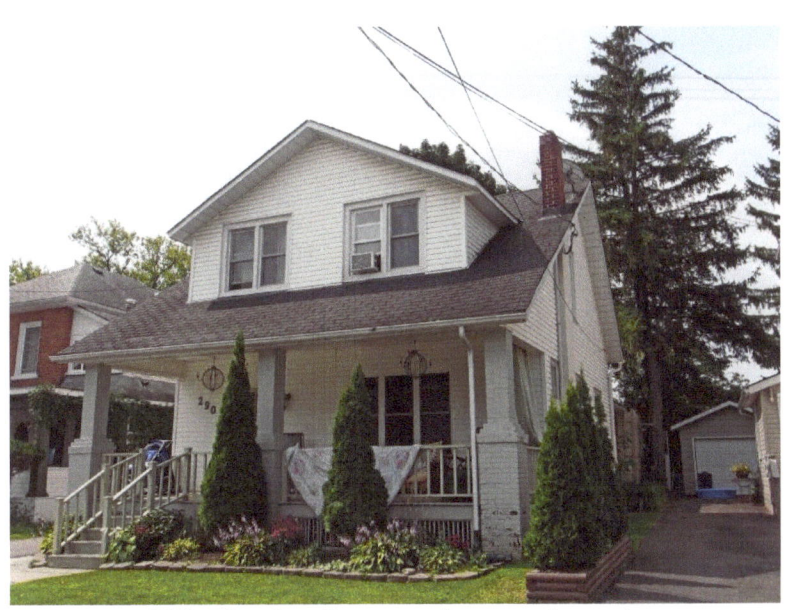

290 Charles Street – dormer in attic

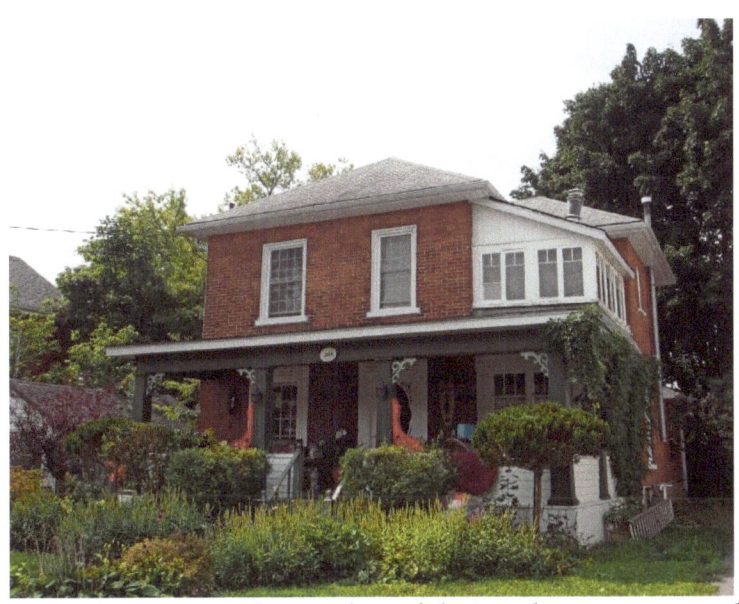

288 Charles Street – hipped roof, bric-a-brac on verandah
posts

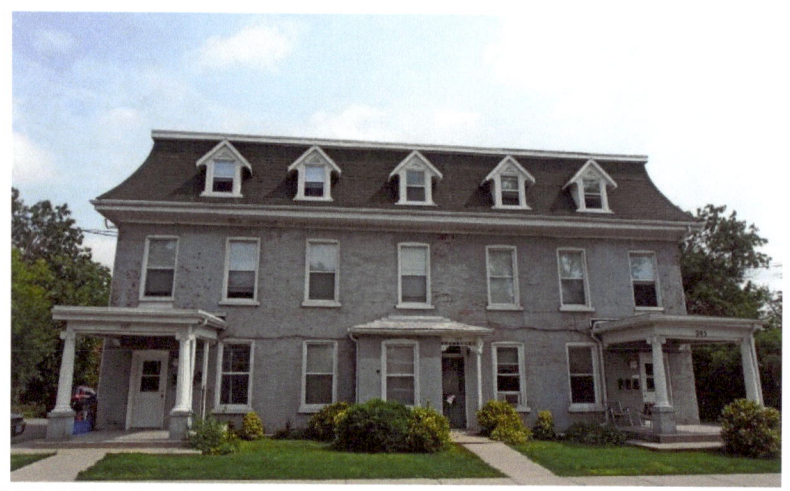

285-289 Charles Street – dormers, Ionic capitals on porch pillars

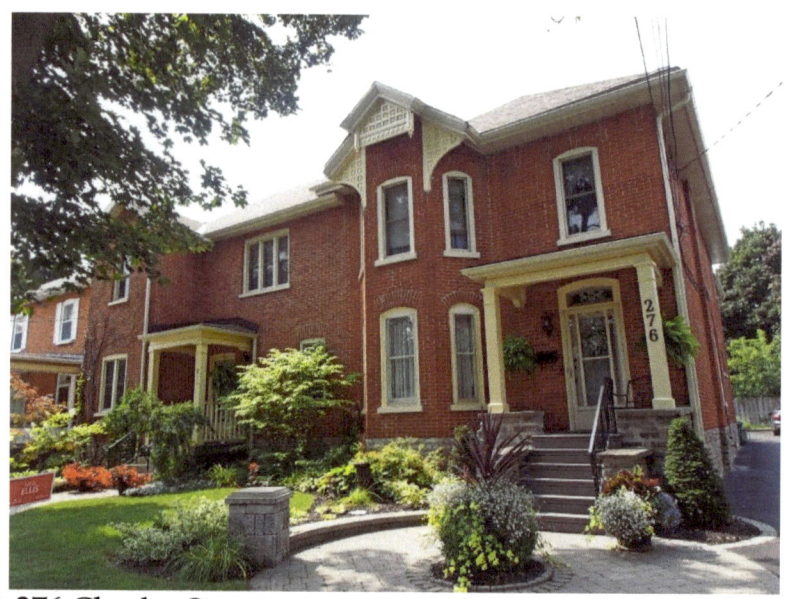

274-276 Charles Street – two-storey bay, fretwork, evidence of former cornice brackets

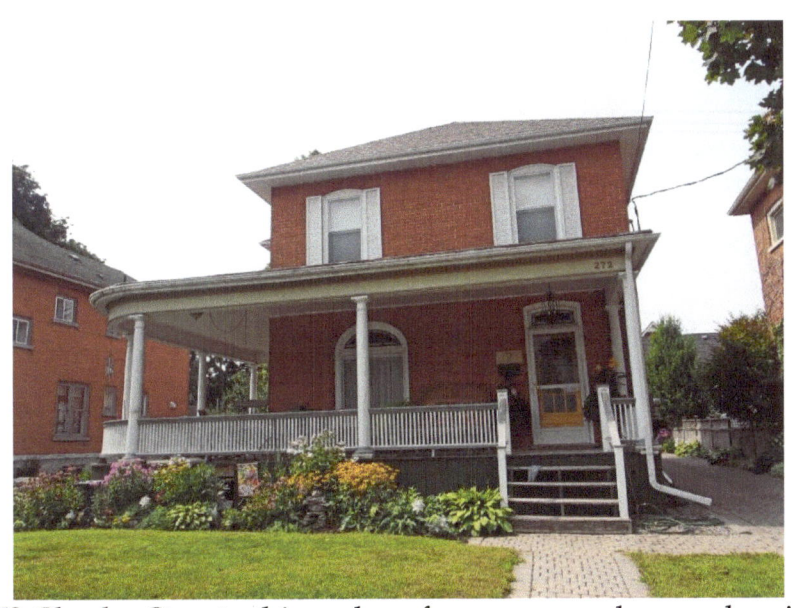

272 Charles Street – hipped roof, wraparound veranda with Doric pillars, open railing

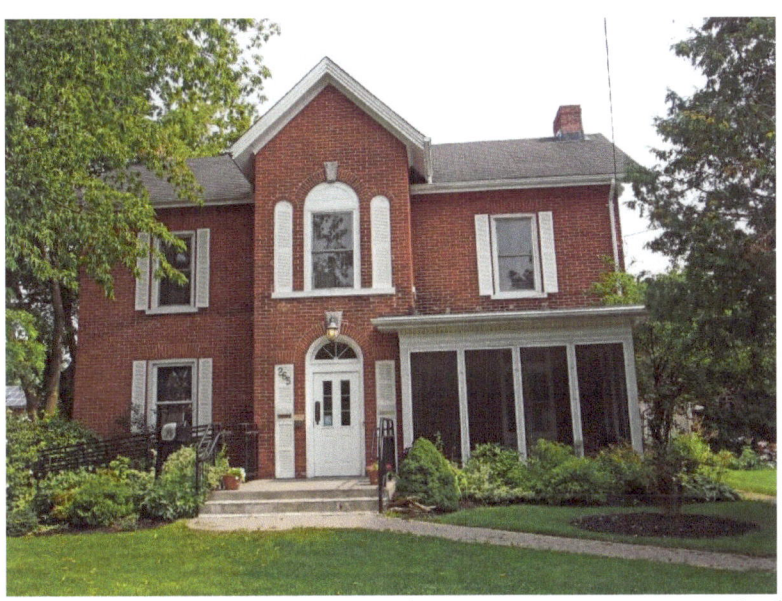

265 Charles Street – two-storey frontispiece, transom window

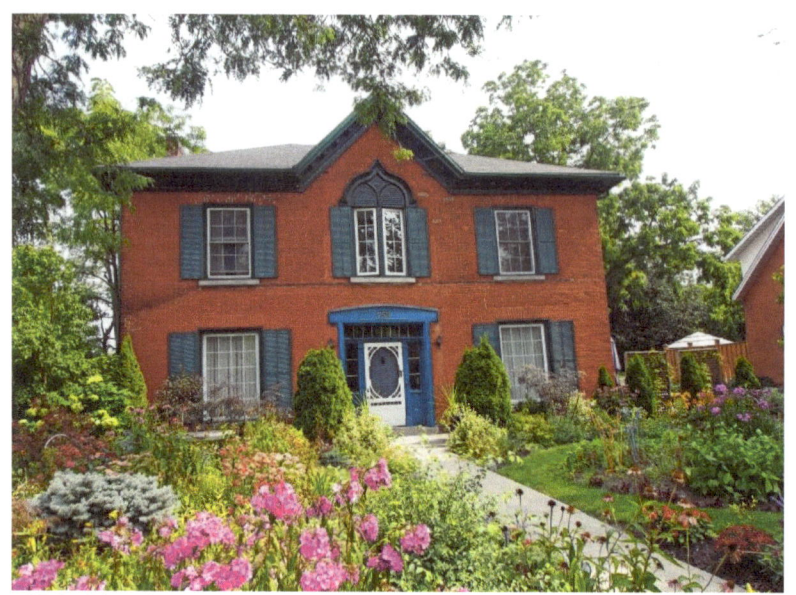

259 Charles Street – sidelights and transom windows

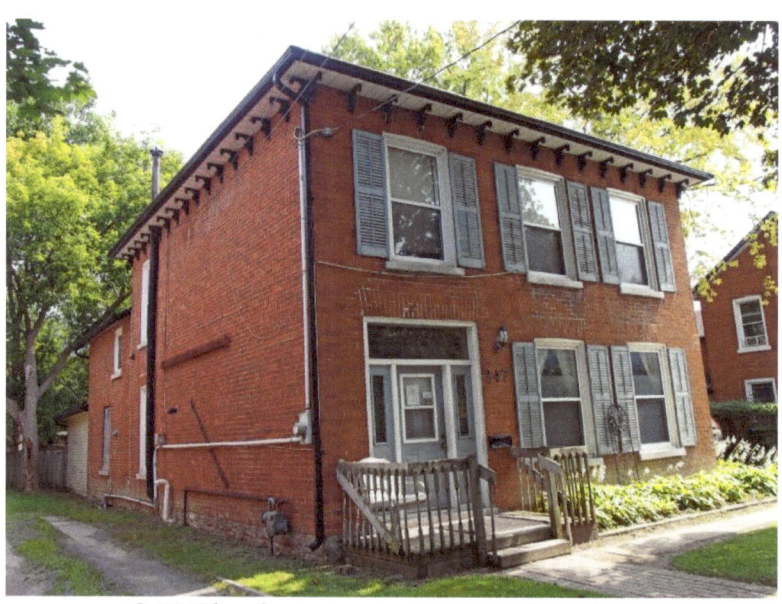

247 Charles Street – cornice brackets

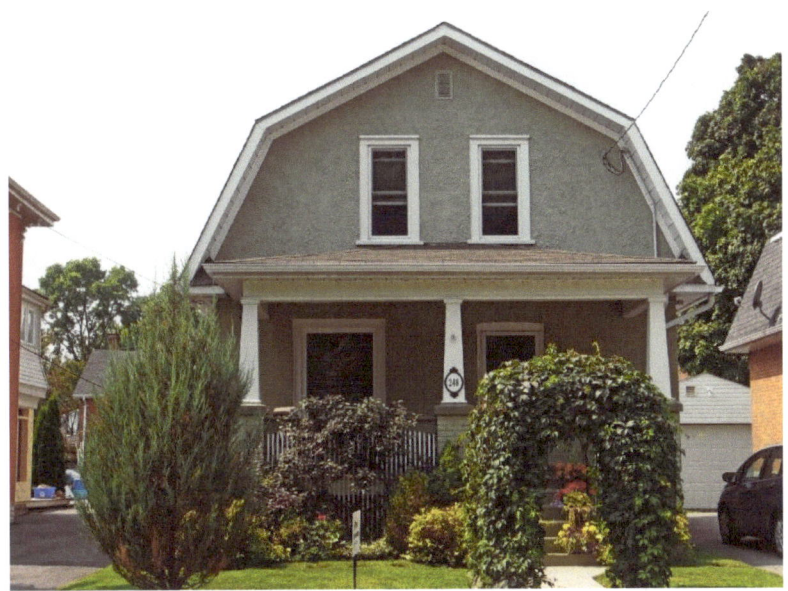

248 Charles Street – Neo-colonial style – gambrel roof

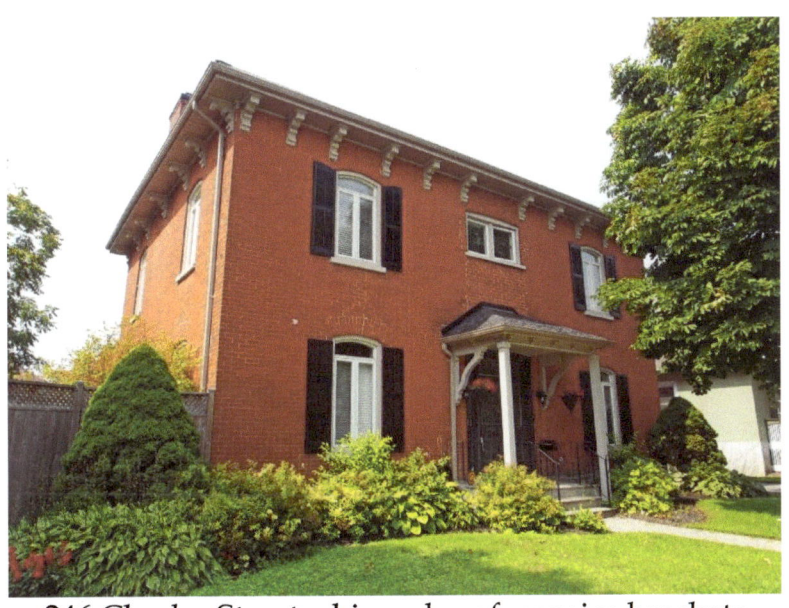

246 Charles Street – hipped roof, cornice brackets

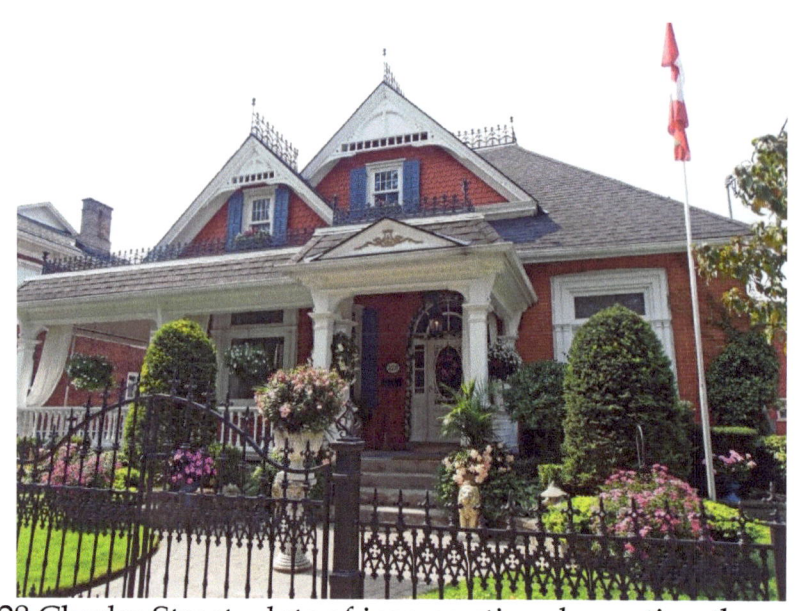

228 Charles Street – lots of iron cresting decorating the roof lines, wraparound verandah with open railing, pillars with ornate capitals, pediment with decorated tympanum, sidelights and transom windows

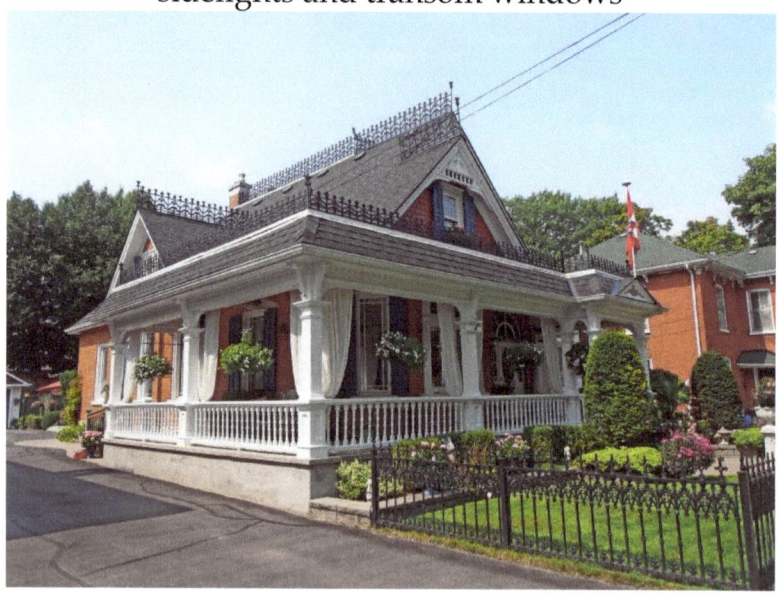

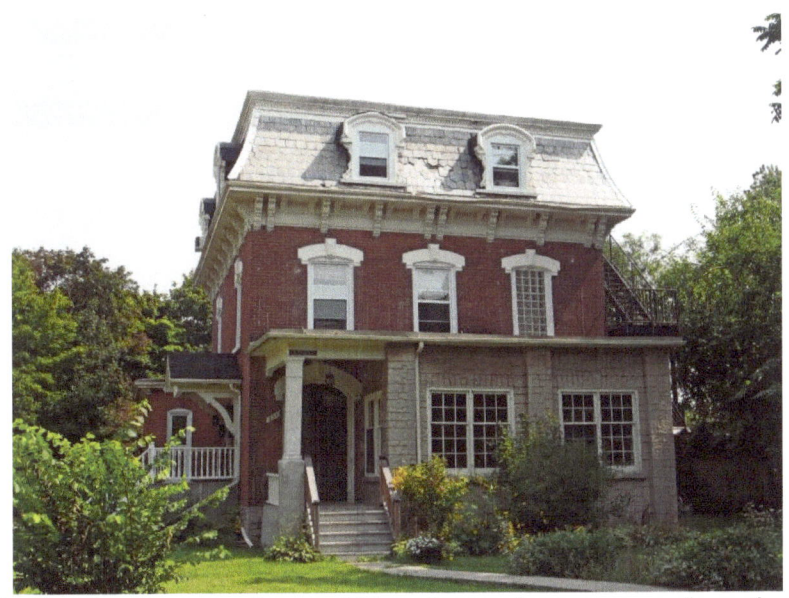

233 Charles Street – Second Empire style – mansard roof with dormers and window hoods, brackets and decorative cornice, keystones

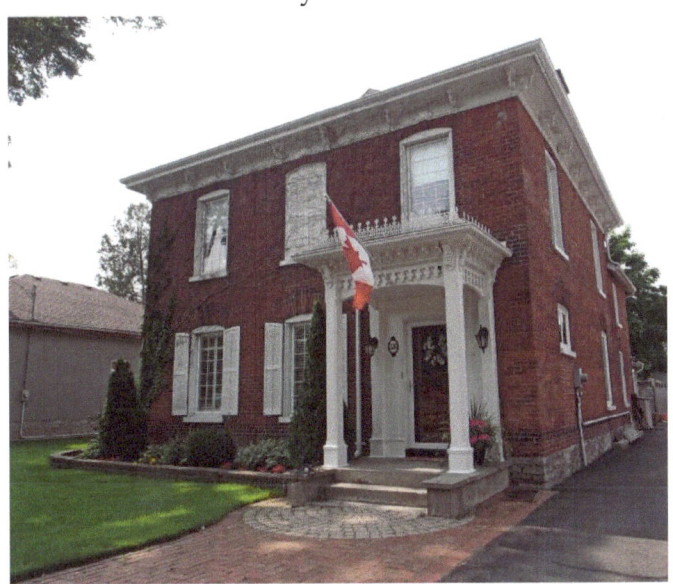

226 Charles Street – hipped roof, cornice brackets, decorative entrance with iron cresting above

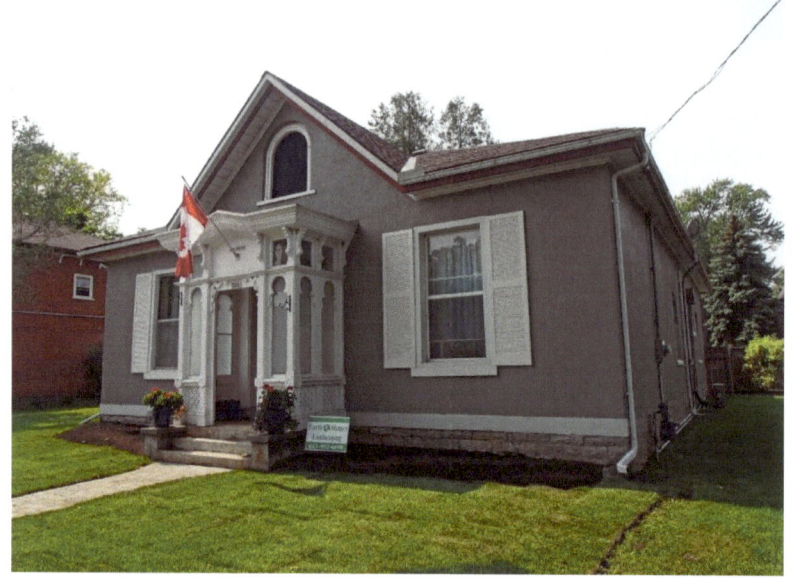

220 Charles Street – Gothic - decorative entrance

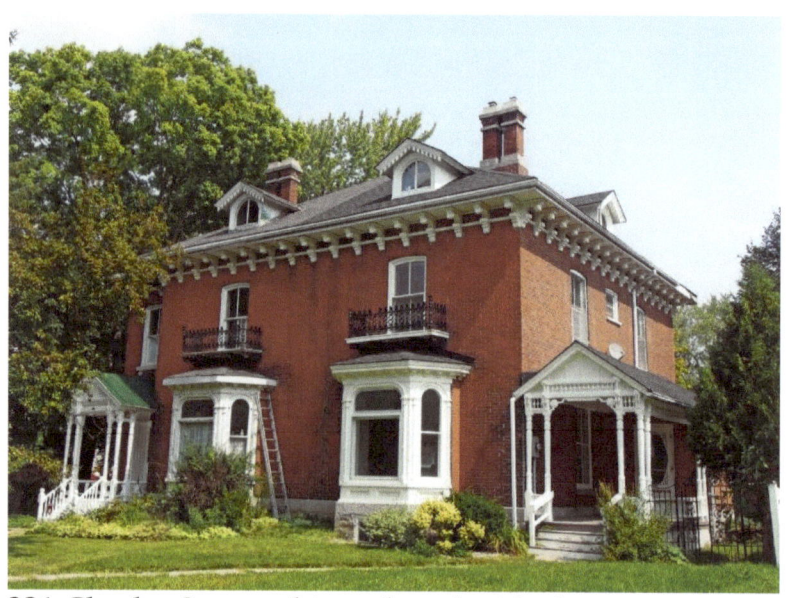

221 Charles Street – hipped roof with dormers, cornice brackets, bay windows with iron cresting above, pediment

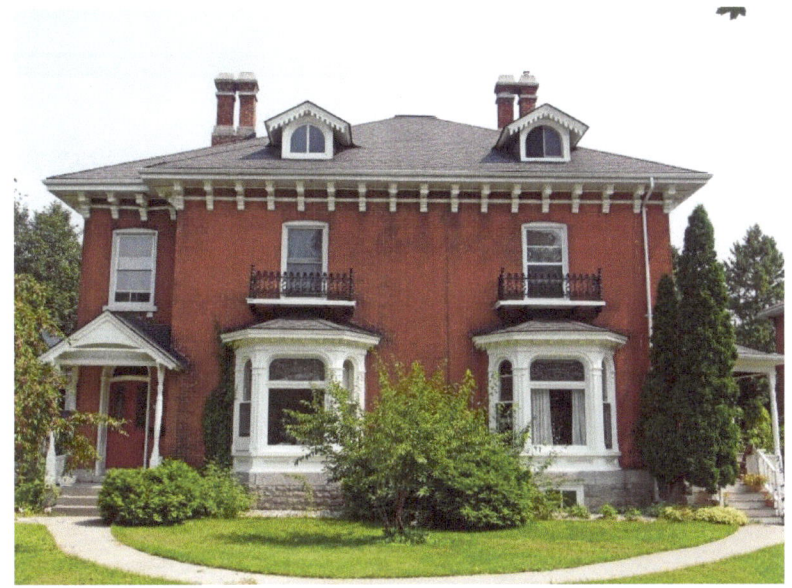

215 Charles Street – same style as 221 Charles Street

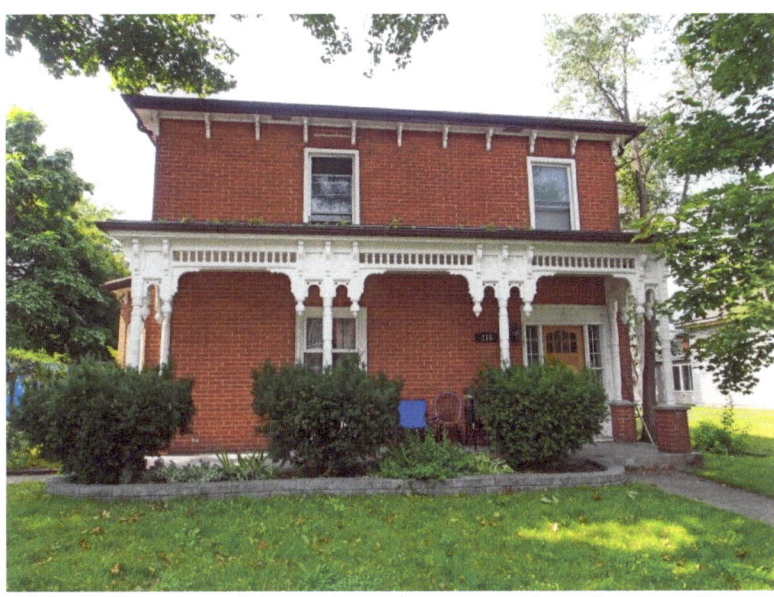

216 Charles Street – hipped roof, cornice brackets, pillars with ornate capitals

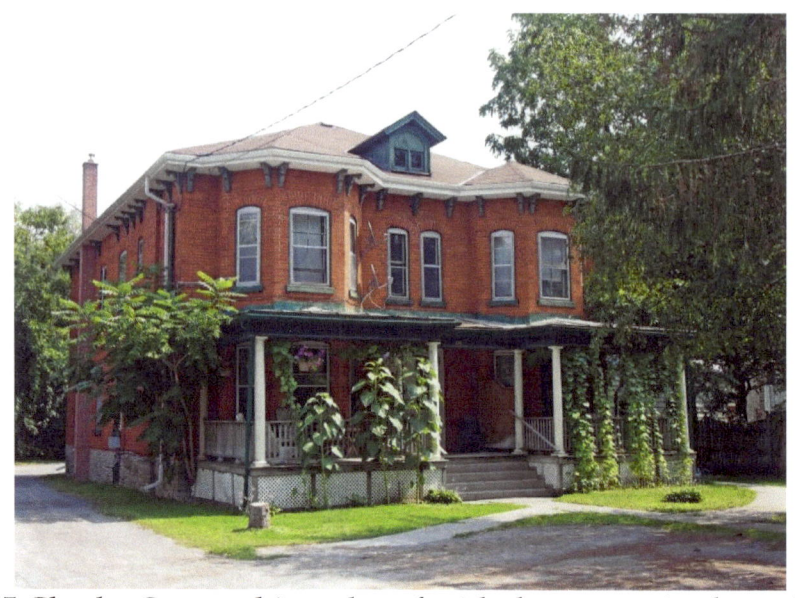

205 Charles Street – hipped roof with dormer, paired cornice brackets, two-storey bay windows

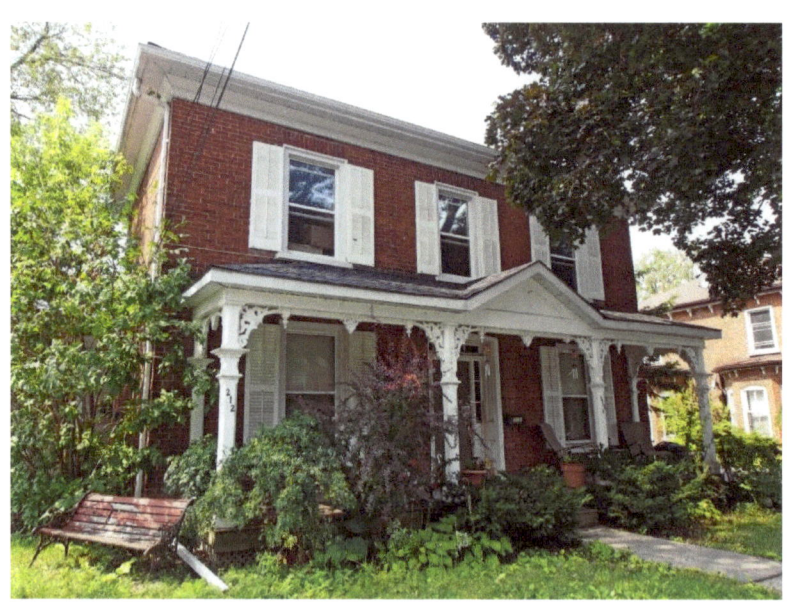

212 Charles Street - pillars with ornate capitals, pediment

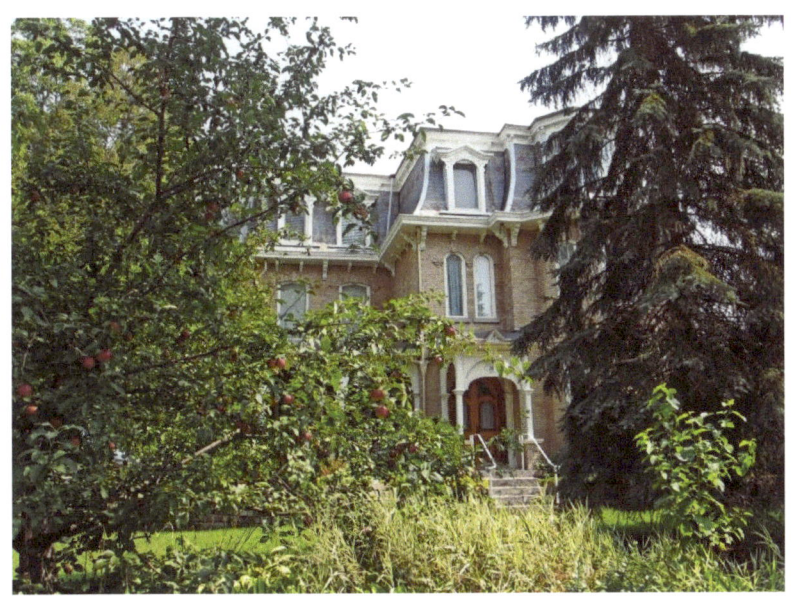

201 Charles Street – Second Empire – mansard roof, window hoods, polychromatic tile work

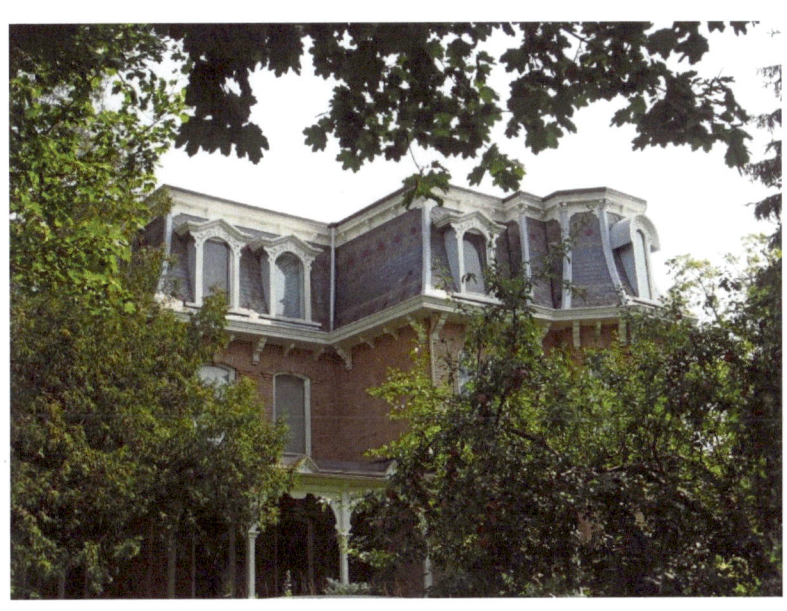

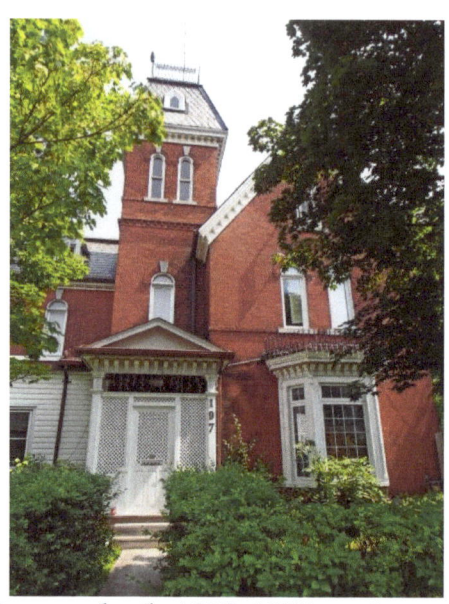

197 Charles Street – built 1872-1873 - mixture of Italianate, Victorian, Second Empire and Gothic styles – mansard roof on 3½-storey tower with small Gothic windows and iron cresting; voussoirs and keystones, dentil molding, bay window with brackets, pediment above door

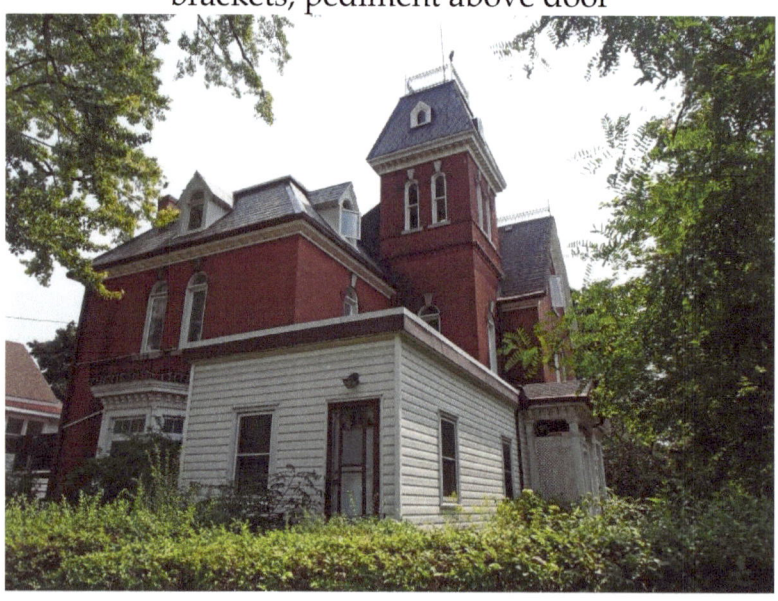

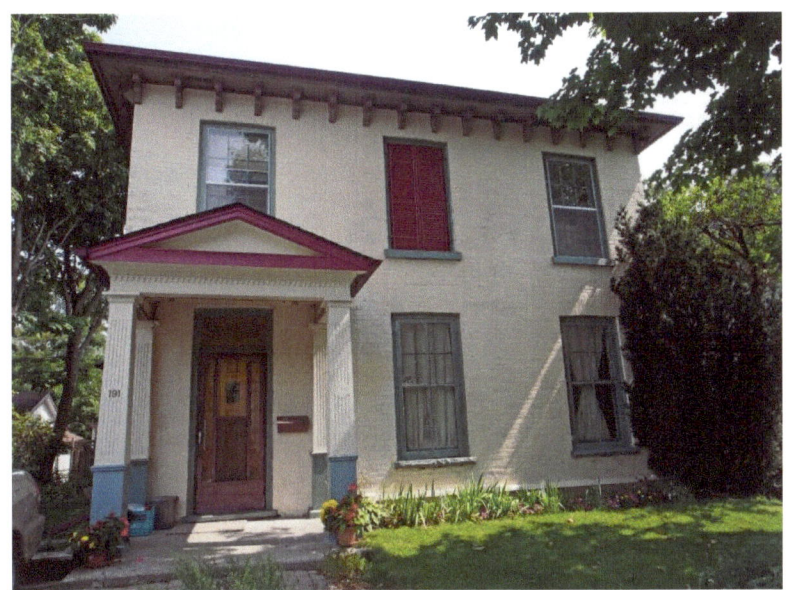

191 Charles Street – built 1872 as a manse for Bridge Street Methodist Church - Victorian family home; the upper floor has two tall windows with a false one in the center; cornice brackets, pediment

188 Charles Street – rectangular bay window, pediment

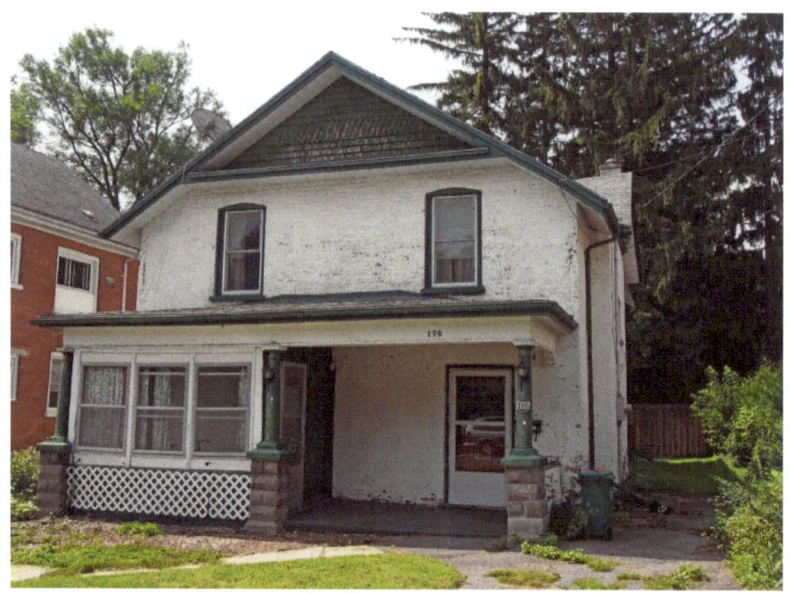

176 Charles Street

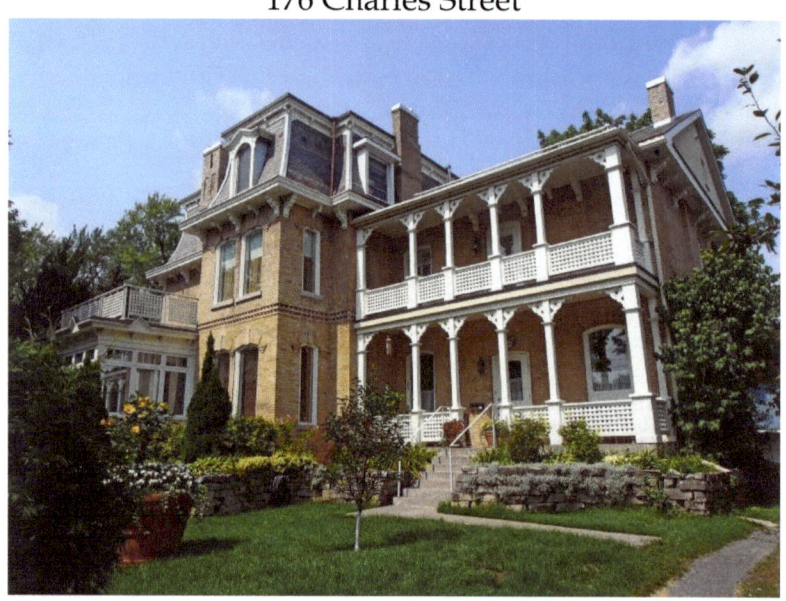

160 Charles Street – Second Empire – mansard roof, dormers with window hoods, polychromatic tile work, two-storey wing with ornate capitals on the two-storey veranda with open railing

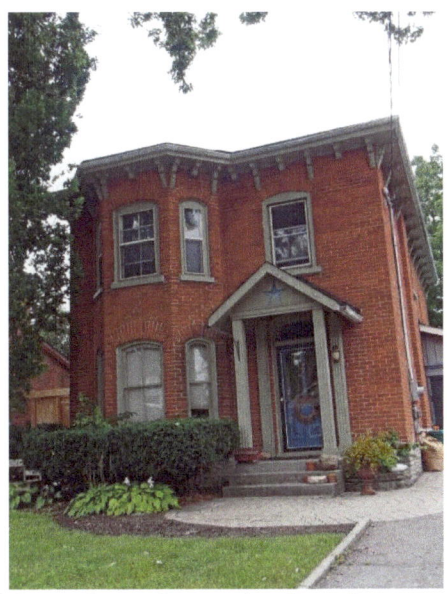

Albert Street – hipped roof, cornice brackets, transom window

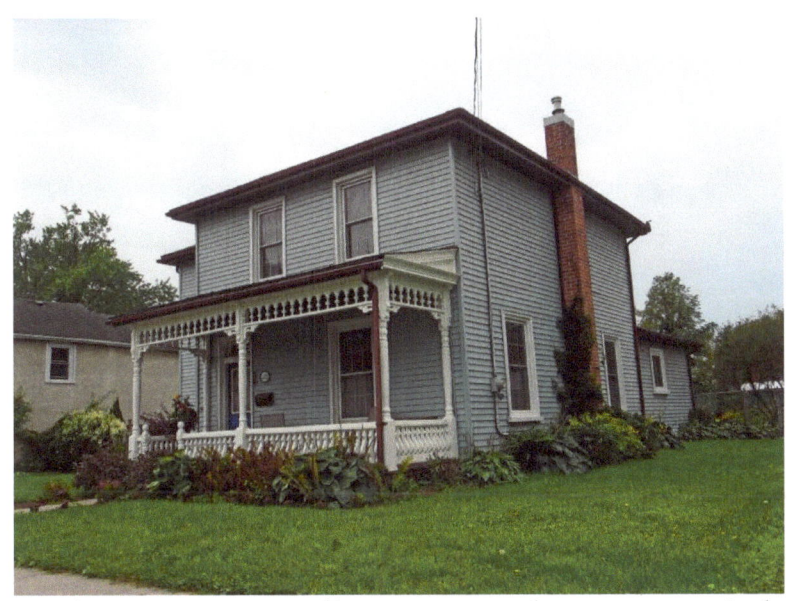

322 Albert Street – spindling on veranda, transom window

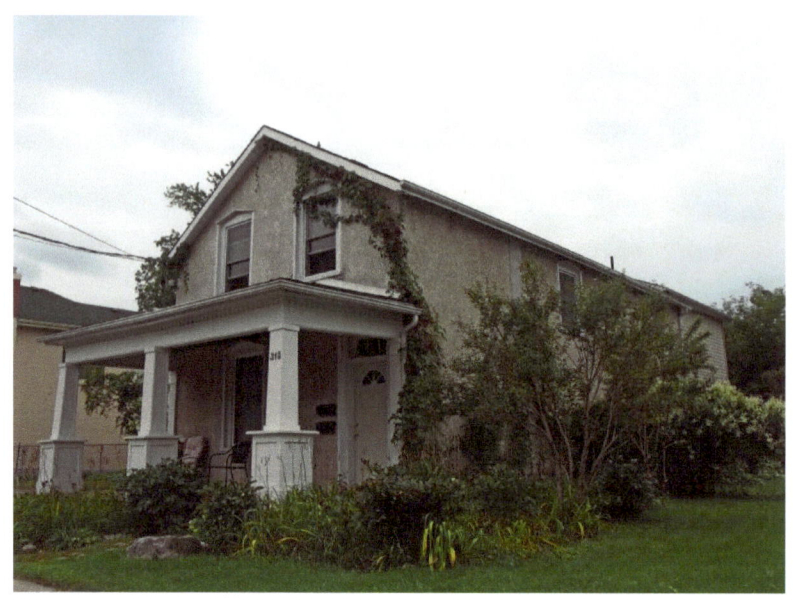

318 Albert Street – transom window

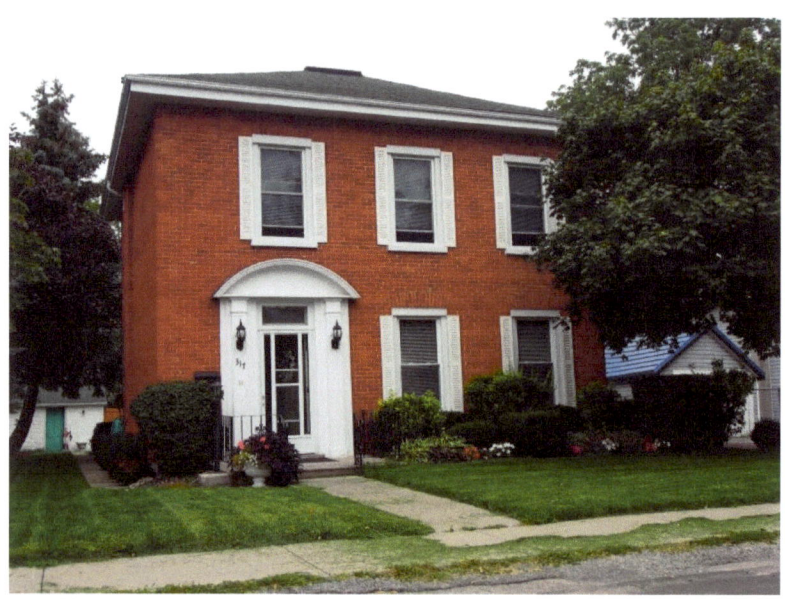

317 Albert Street – hipped roof, transom window, engaged
columns surrounding door

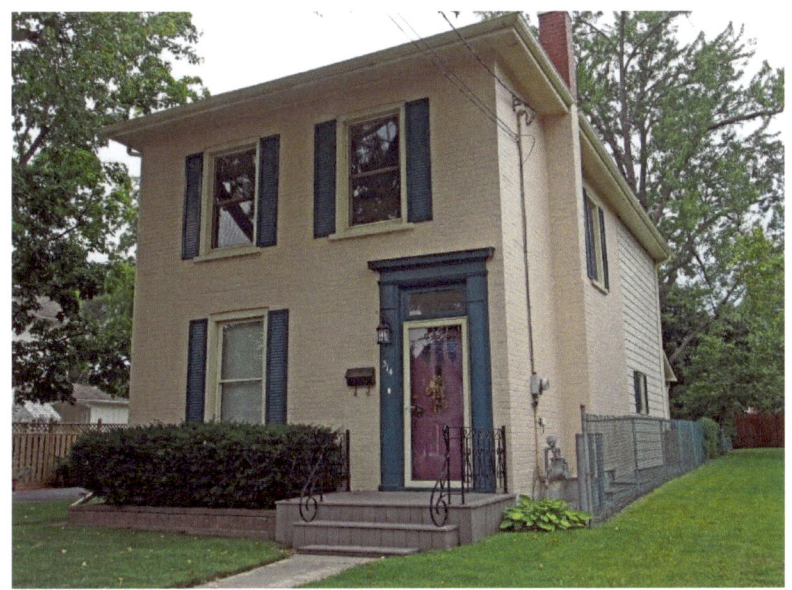

314 Albert Street - transom window, engaged columns surrounding door

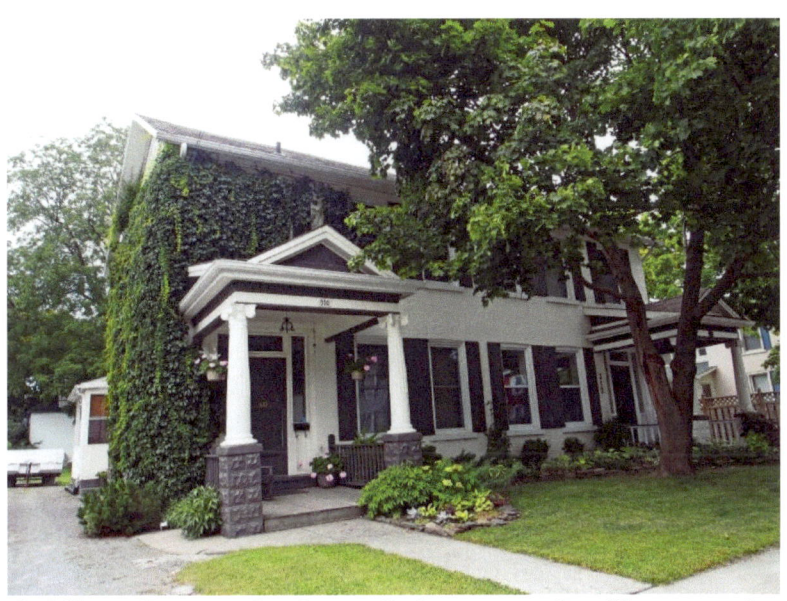

310 Albert Street – Ionic capitals on porch pillars on piers, pediment, sidelights and transom window

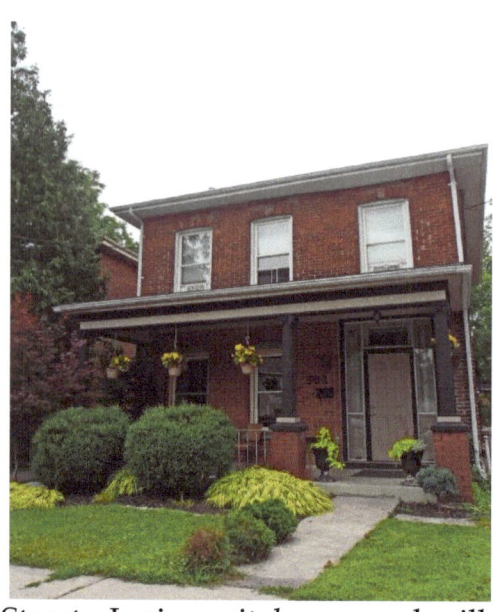

302 Albert Street - Ionic capitals on porch pillars on brick piers, sidelights and transom window

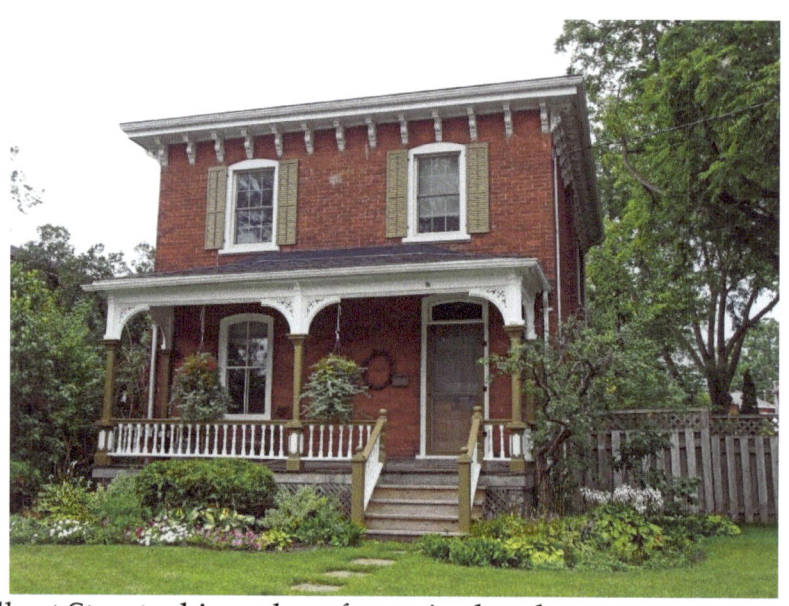

Albert Street – hipped roof, cornice brackets, ornate capitals on veranda pillars, open railing, transom window

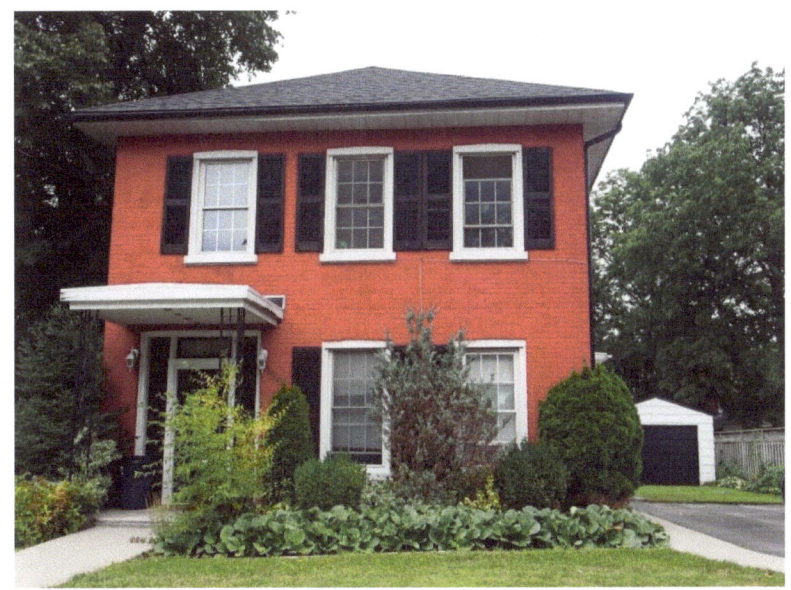

295 Albert Street – hipped roof, transom window

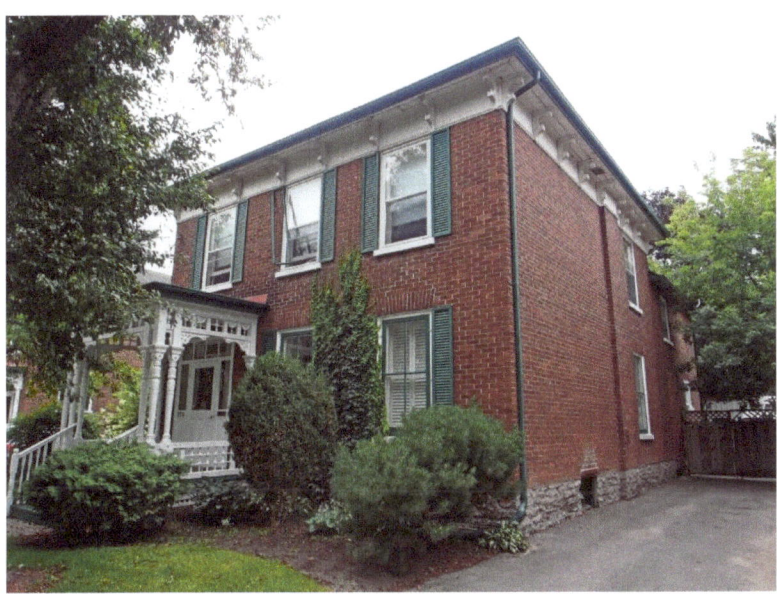

250 Albert Street – hipped roof, cornice brackets, ornate
entrance with open railing

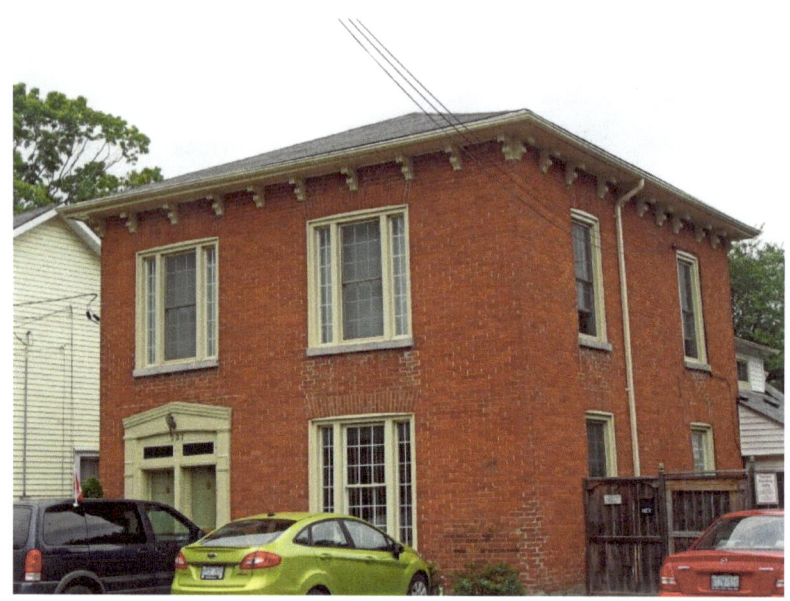

237 Albert Street – hipped roof, cornice brackets, voussoirs

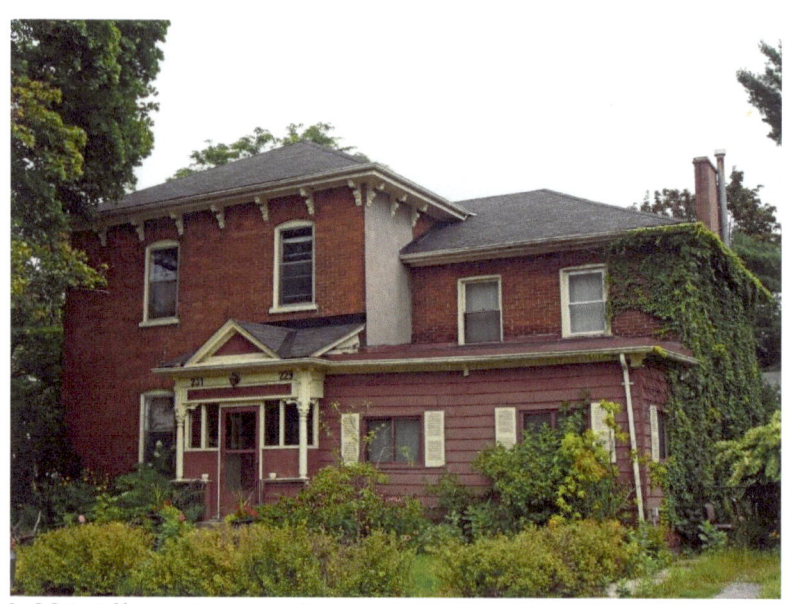

229-231 Albert Street – hipped roof, cornice brackets, ornate capitals on porch pillars

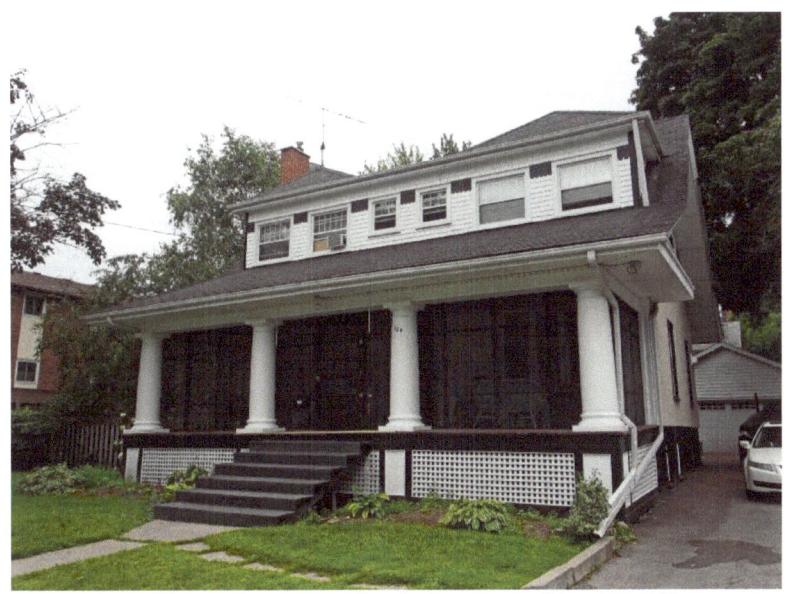

224 Albert Street – shed dormer, Doric pillars

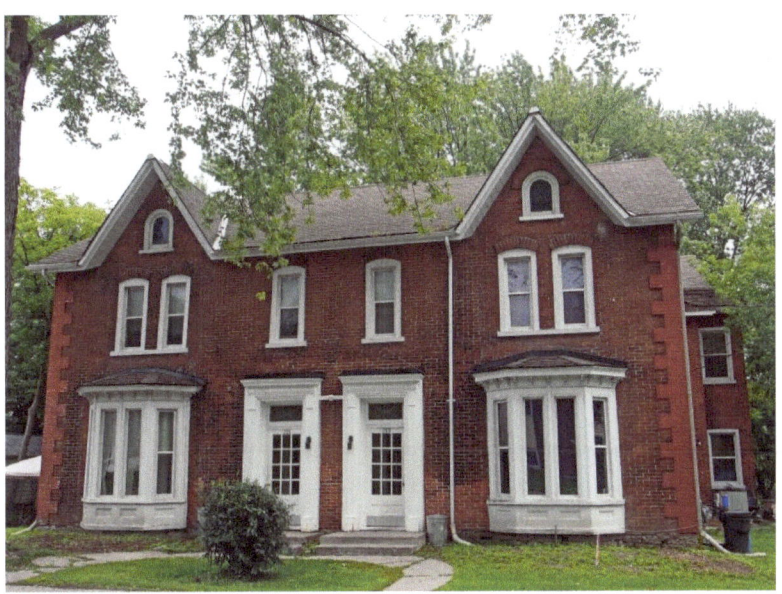

219-221 Albert Street – Gothic, bay windows, corner quoins, voussoirs over windows, transom windows above doors

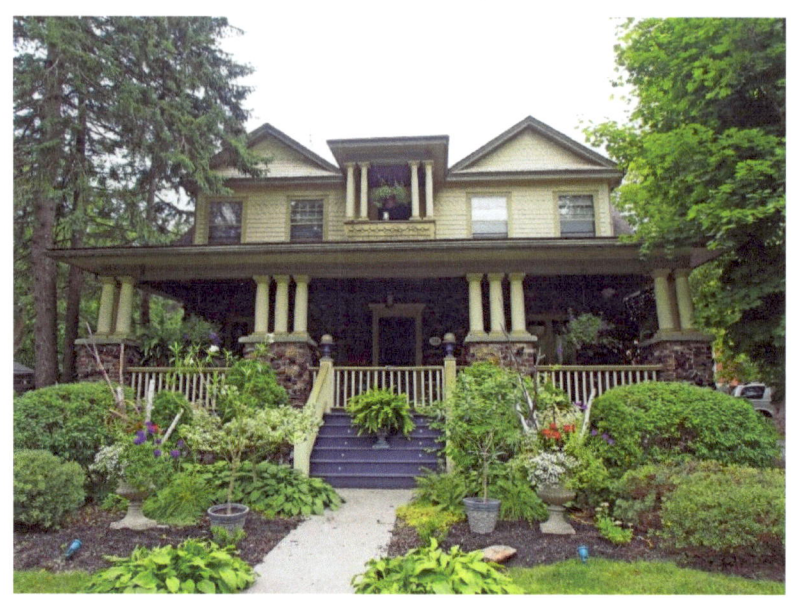

216 Albert Street – Doric pillars on brick piers, matching pillars on second floor balcony, open railing on veranda

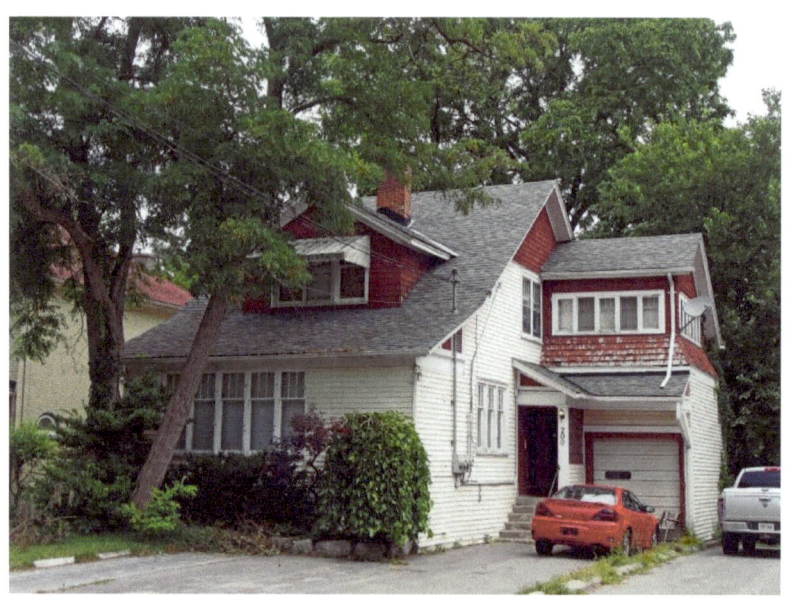

209 Albert Street - dormer

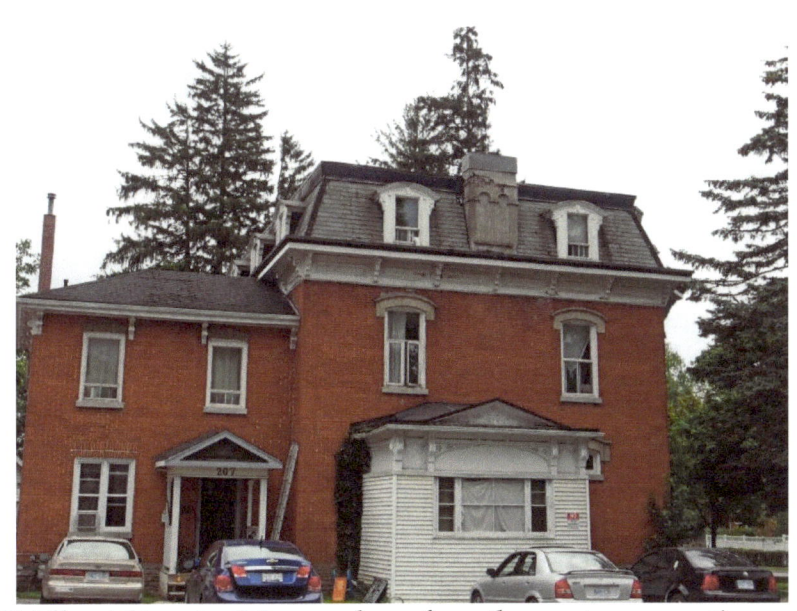

207 Albert Street – Mansard roof on three-storey section with hooded dormers; hipped roof on two-storey wing; cornice brackets

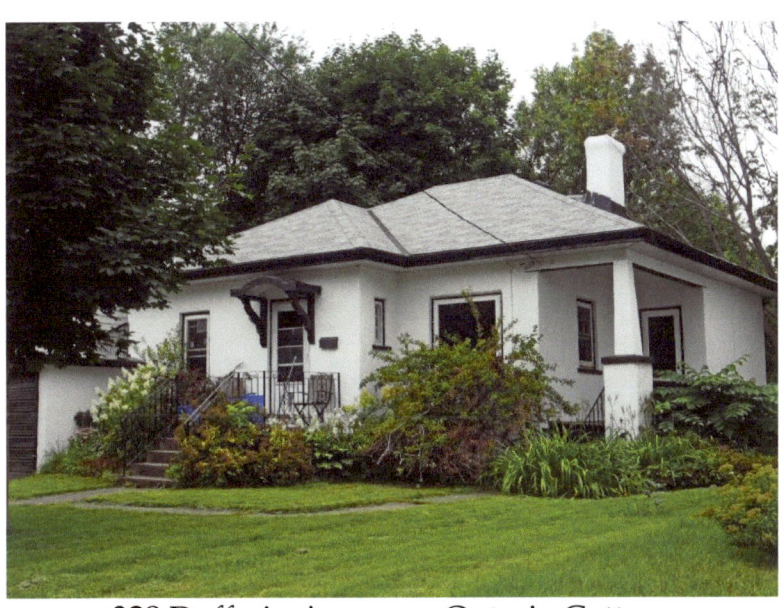

328 Dufferin Avenue – Ontario Cottage

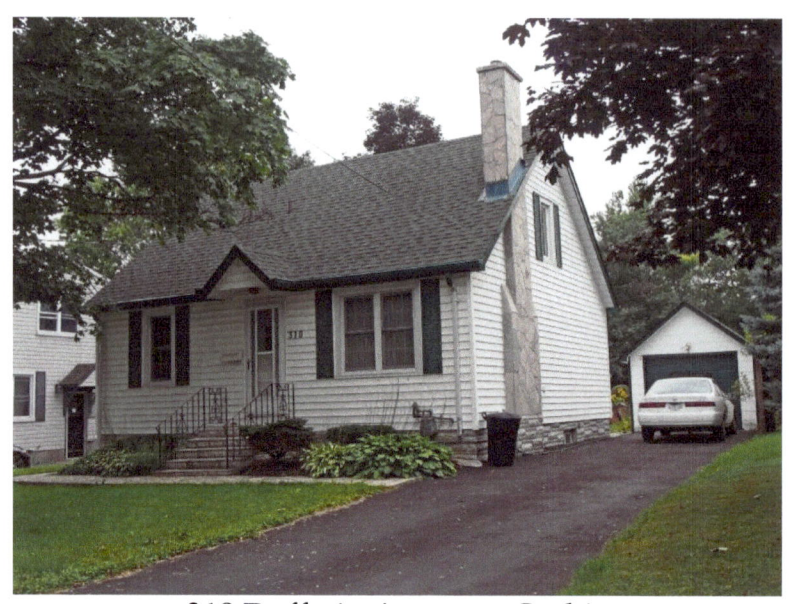

310 Dufferin Avenue - Gothic

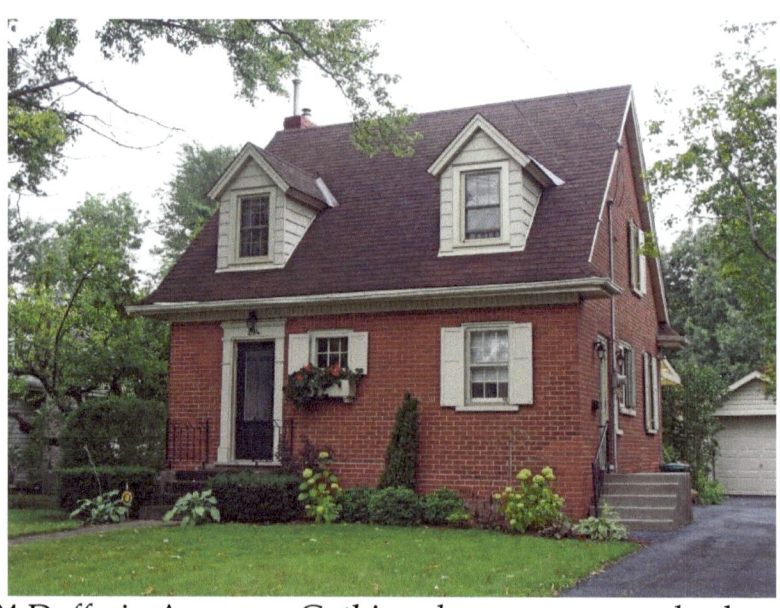

294 Dufferin Avenue – Gothic – dormers, engaged columns around door

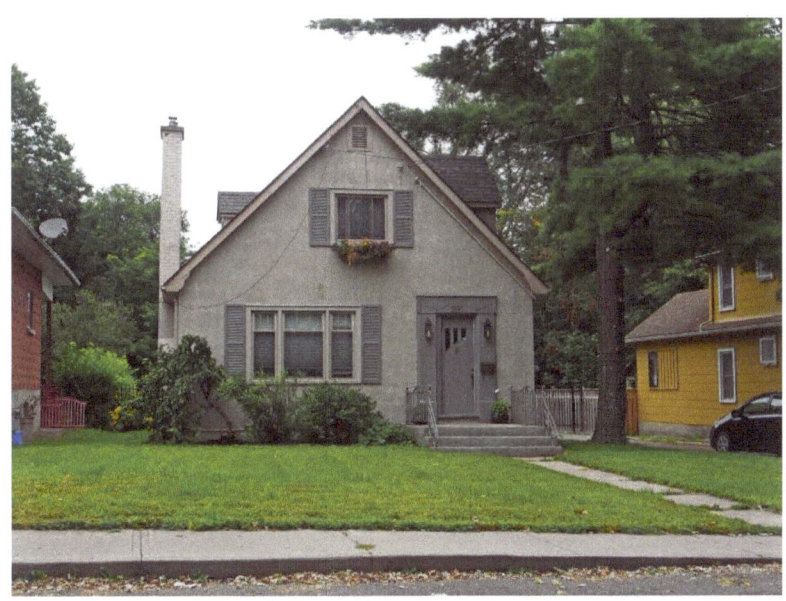

291 Dufferin Avenue

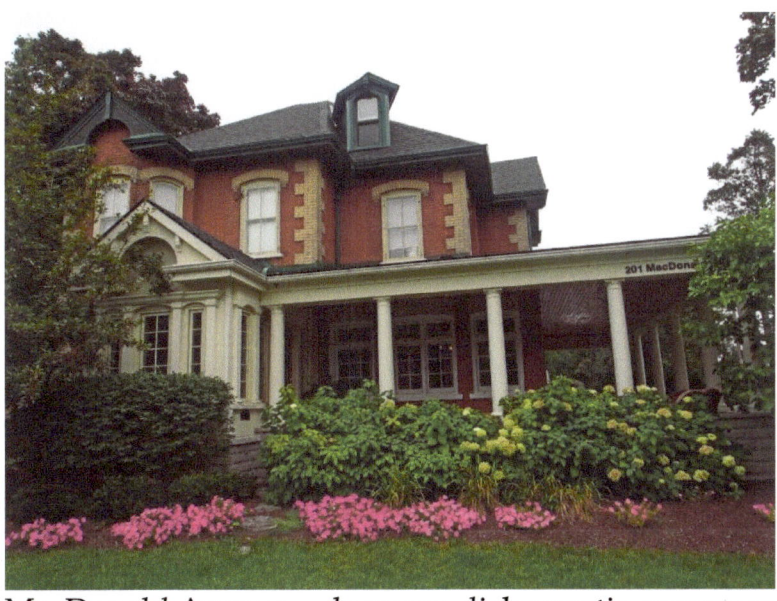

201 MacDonald Avenue – dormers, dichromatic corner quoins and voussoirs, Doric pillars on wraparound veranda, enclosed entrance with engaged pillars, pediment

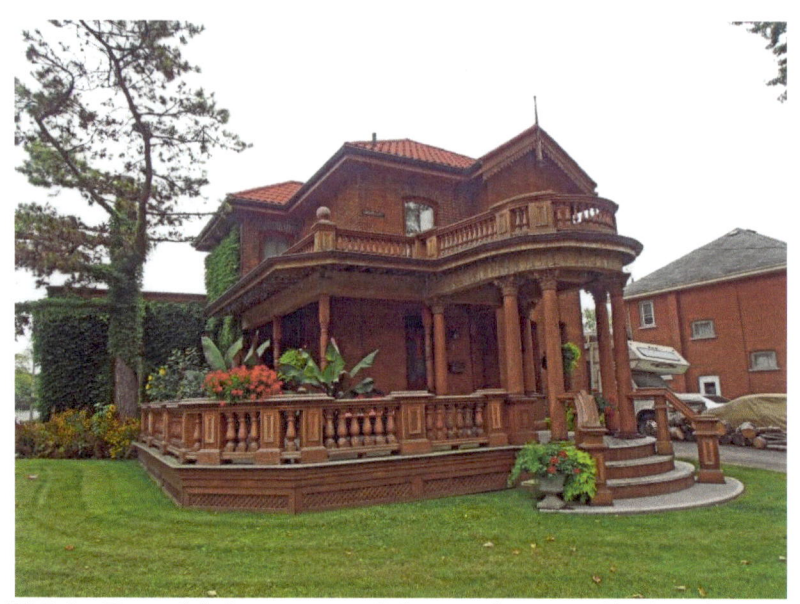

199 MacDonald Avenue – elaborately spindled railings on both lower and upper wraparound verandahs, Corinthian pillars, finial on gable

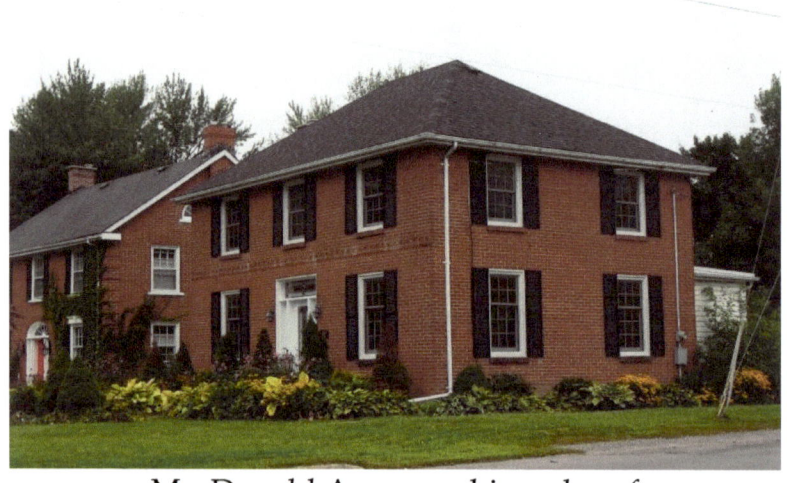

MacDonald Avenue – hipped roof

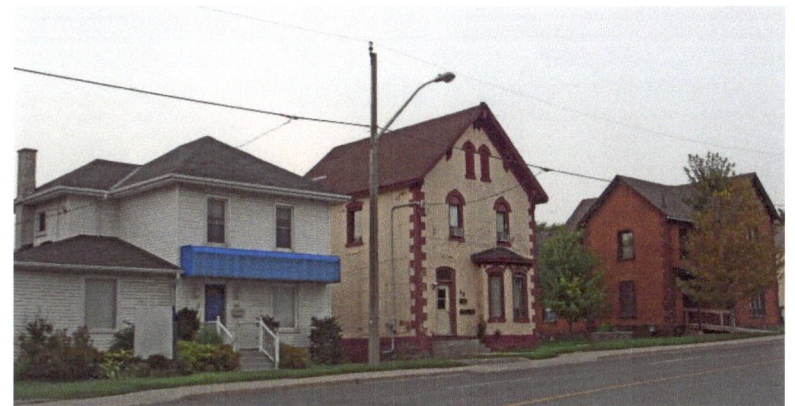

46-48 MacDonald Avenue – corner quoins, bay window

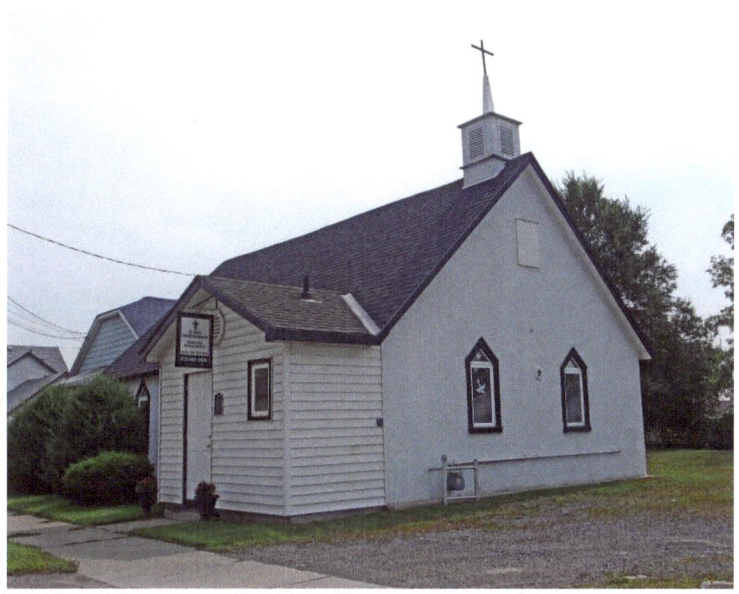

St. Paul Street – St. Paul's Anglican Church - cupola

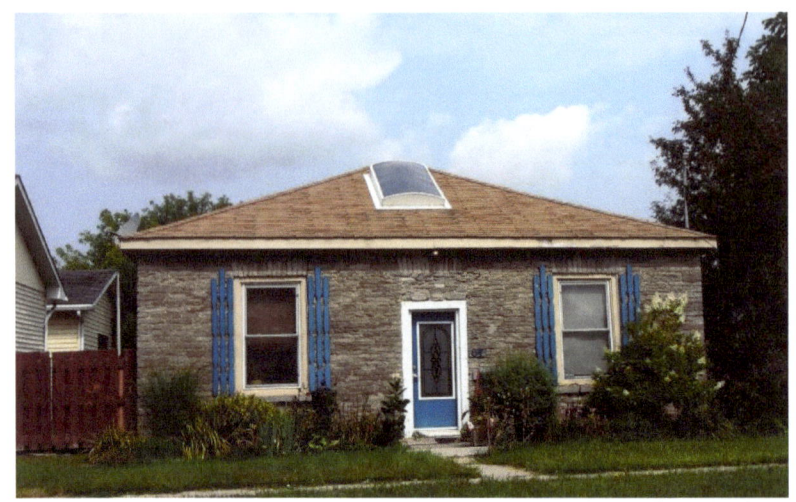

64 St. Paul Street – Ontario Cottage – hipped roof, cobblestone

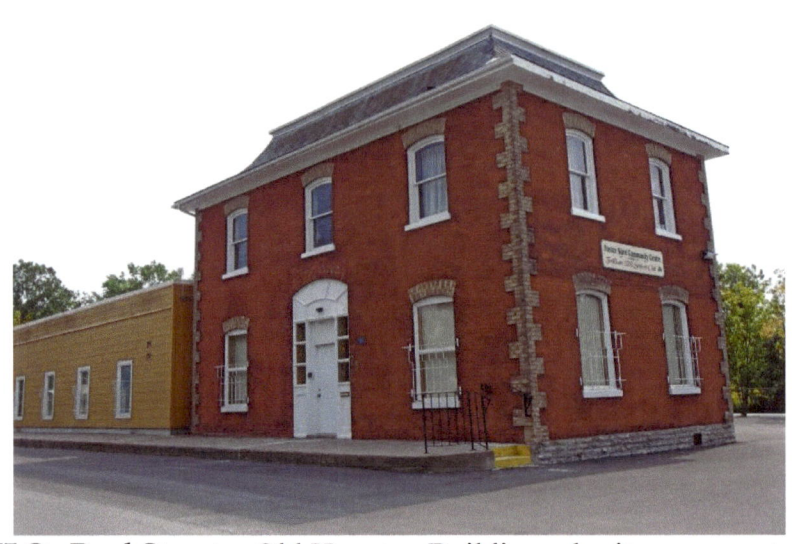

75 St. Paul Street – Old Houston Building – heritage property -
Foster Ward Community Centre – dichromatic corner quoins
and voussoirs

Architectural Terms

Bay Window: A window that projects out from a wall, in a semicircular, rectangular, or polygonal design. Used frequently in Gothic and Victorian designs. Example: 215 Charles Street, Page 34	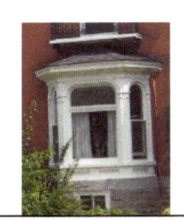
Brackets: a decorative or weight-bearing structural element which forms a right angle with one side against a wall and the other under a projecting surface such as an eave or roof. Example: 215 Charles Street, Page 34	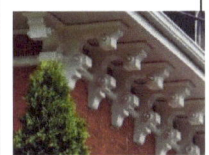
Capital: The uppermost finish or decoration on a column. An Ionic column has a small base, a thin elegant shaft, and a capital composed of volutes which are carved whirls or twists that take the form of a scroll. Example: 234 Ann Street, Page 17	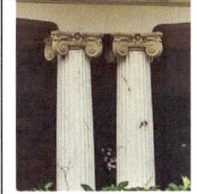 Ionic
A Doric column is characterized by a plain column with no base, a shaft with twenty flutings, and a simple capital with a simple entablature. Example: 216 Albert Street, Page 48	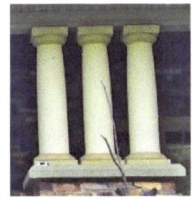 Doric
A Corinthian column is characterized by a rounded capital decorated with acanthus leaves and a square abacus (the uppermost portion of a capital directly below the entablature) on tall slender columns. Example: 199 MacDonald Avenue, Page 52	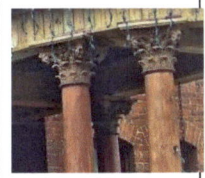 Corinthian

Cobblestone architecture: Refers to the use of cobblestones embedded in mortar as a method for erecting walls on houses and commercial buildings. Example: 153 William Street, Page 6	
Cornice: originally the wooden overhang of the roof. With the use of stone, brick, iron and steel, the cornice is any horizontal moulded projection at the top of a building. They can be very decorative. Example: 233 Charles Street, Page 31	
Course: continuous horizontal row or layer of stone or brick. Example: 253-257 Ann Street, Page 20	
Cupola: A domed or curved roof rising from a building as a decorative element. Example: St. Paul Street, Page 53	
Dentil Moulding: an even series of rectangles used as ornamental decoration in cornices. Example: 197 Charles Street, Page 38	
Dichromatic brickwork: the use of two colours of brick, tile or slate to decorate a façade. Example: 201 MacDonald Avenue, Page 51	

Dormer: (French for "sleep") a gable end window that pierces through the plane of a sloping roof surface to create usable space in the top floor or attic of a building by adding headroom. Example: 285-289 Charles Street, Page 27	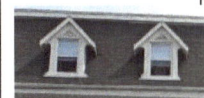
Entrance: The entrance encompasses the doorway and the inner vestibule or, in residential architecture, the covered porch. Example: 220 Charles Street, Page 33	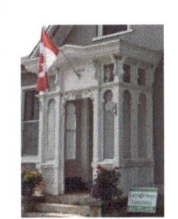
Fretwork: interlaced decorative design resembling a bracket Example: 274-276 Charles Street, Page 28	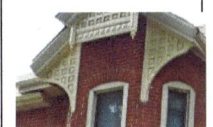
Frontispiece: a portion of the façade of a building, usually a centred doorway that is slightly raised from the rest of the building, usually has extensive ornamentation. Frontispieces are usually Classical in design with white columned porches. Example: 184 William Street, Page 10	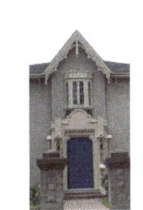
Gable: the triangular portion of a wall between the edges of a sloping roof. Example: 264 Ann Street, Page 21	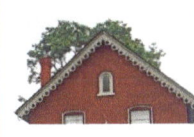

Gambrel Roof: a symmetrical two-sided roof with two slopes on each side; the upper slope is positioned at a shallow angle, while the lower slope is steep. It is similar to a mansard roof, but a gambrel has vertical gable ends instead of being hipped at the four corners of the building. Example: 248 Charles Street, Page 30	
Hipped Roof: a roof where all sides slope downwards to the walls with no gables. Example: 272 Charles Street, Page 28	
Iron Cresting: A decorative ornament along the top of a roof. Iron cresting was popular in the Baroque era and also in Italianate, Victorian, Second Empire and Queen Anne styles of architecture. Example: 215 Charles Street, Page 34	
Keystones and Voussoirs: a voussoir is a wedge-shaped element used in building an arch. A keystone is the central stone that locks all the stones into position, allowing the arch to bear weight. A keystone is often enlarged and embellished. Example: 197 Charles Street, Page 38	

Mansard Roof: This style was popularized by Francois Mansart (1598-1666), an accomplished architect of the French Baroque period and especially fashionable during the Second French Empire (1852-1870). This roof is almost flat on the top section, with two slopes on each of its sides with the lower slope at a steeper angle than the upper, and has dormer windows. Example: 201 Charles Street, Page 37	
Oriel Window - These small areas were originally set into walls and galleries for the purpose of private prayer. Over time, any projecting window or area on an upper floor was called an oriel. Example: 234 Ann Street, Page 17	
Pediment: a triangular section above the door or portico, usually supported by columns. The inside of the triangle is called the tympanum. Example: 228 Charles Street, Page 32	
Pilaster: a slightly projecting column built into or applied to the face of a wall for additional structural support. Example: 253-257 Ann Street, Page 20	
Quoin: masonry blocks at the corner of a wall, often a decorative feature, usually larger or of a different colour than the rest of the wall. Example: 75 St. Paul Street, Page 54	

Sidelight: a vertical window that flanks a door, and is often used to emphasize the importance of a primary entrance. **Transom Window:** the light above the doorway, also called a fanlight. Example: 259 Charles Street, Page 29	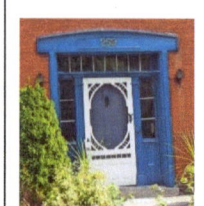
Tower: A circular, square, or octagonal vertical structure higher than the surrounding structure that is usually part of an existing building and is created either for extra defense or for a specific purpose such as a clock or a bell tower. Example: 224 Ann Street, Page 18	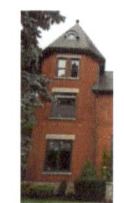
Verge board and Finial: also called bargeboards – hang from the projecting end of a roof and are often elaborately carved and ornamented. **Finial:** ornament added to the top of a gable, pinnacle, canopy or spire – a Gothic element. Example: 201 William Street, Page 12	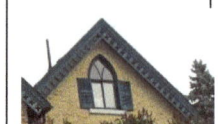
Window Hood: A **hood** is the piece found above window openings, usually of an ornate design, and covers the top third of the opening. Hoods are commonly placed above arched or curved openings on both windows and doors. Example: 233 Charles Street, Page 31	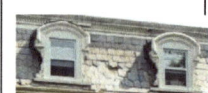

Building Styles

Arts and Crafts: The overlying theme - the house was based on the function of the house. Rooms were oriented to take advantage of the movement of the sun for warmth and light during daylight hours. Side entrances allowed for useable space on the front facade for light or garden use. Arts and Crafts houses have many of these features: wood, stone or stucco siding; low-pitched roof; wide eaves with triangular brackets; exposed roof rafters; porch with thick square or round columns; stone porch supports; exterior chimney made with stone; open floor plans with few hallways; many windows, some with stained or leaded glass; beamed ceilings; dark wood wainscoting and moldings; built-in cabinets, shelves, and seating. Example: 165 William Street, Page 8	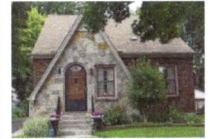
Edwardian, 1900-1930 – This style bridges the ornate and elaborate styles of the Victorian era and the simplified styles of the 20th century. Edwardian Classicism provided simple, balanced facades, simple rooflines, dormer windows, large front porches, and smooth brick surfaces. Voussoirs and keystones are used sparingly and are understated. Finials and cresting are absent. Cornice brackets and braces are block-like and openings have flat arches or plain stone lintels. Example: 188 William Street, Page 11	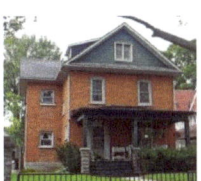

Gothic Revival, 1830-1890 – These decorative buildings have sharply-pitched gables with highly detailed verge boards, pointed-arch window openings, and dichromatic brickwork. It is a common style in Ontario. Example: 264 Ann Street, Page 21	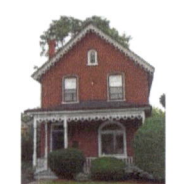
Italianate, 1850-1900 – A two story rectangular building with a mild hip roof, a projecting frontispiece, and generous eaves with ornate cornice brackets was the basis of the style; often there are large sash windows, quoins, ornate detailing on the windows, belvederes and wraparound verandahs. Italianate commercial buildings often have cast iron cresting and elegant window surrounds. Example: 231 William Street, Page 15	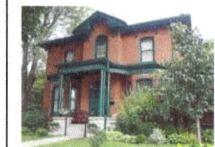
Neo-colonial (also Colonial Revival, Georgian Revival or Neo-Georgian) architecture seeks to revive elements of architectural style of American colonial architecture of the period around the Revolutionary War which drew strongly from Georgian architecture of Great Britain. Architecture from the 18th and early 19th centuries in Ontario includes a wide assortment of detailing and ornament applied to a design centered around the fireplace and the source of water. Structures are typically two stories, have a symmetrical front facade with elaborate front doorways, often with decorative crown pediments, fanlights, and sidelights, symmetrical windows flanking the front entrance, often in pairs or threes, and columned porches. Example: 248 Charles Street, Page 30	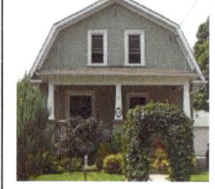

Ontario Cottage - one or one-and-a-half story buildings with a cottage or hip roof. The cottage roof is an equal hip roof where each hip extends to a point in the center of the roof. The hip roof has a long hip in the center. The Ontario Cottage is the vernacular design of the Regency Cottage which generally has a more ornate doorway and a partial or full verandah surrounding it. The roof can have a dormer, a belvedere, and generally two chimneys. Example: 278 Ann Street, Page 22	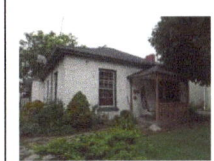
Queen Anne, 1885-1900 – This style is distinguished by an irregular outline featuring a combination of an offset tower, broad gables, projecting two-storey bays, verandahs, multi-sloped roofs, and tall, decorative chimneys. A mixture of brick and wood is common. Windows often have one large single-paned bottom sash and small panes in the upper sash. Example: 234 Ann Street, Page 17	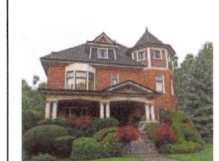
Second Empire, 1860-1880 – The mansard roof is the most noteworthy feature of this style and is evidence of the French origins. Projecting central towers and one or two-storey bays can also be present. Example: 233 Charles Street, Page 31	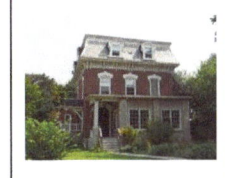
Tudor Revival – exposed timbers with stucco infill, multi-paned windows. Example: 161 William Street, Page 7	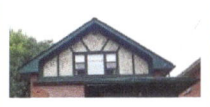

Vernacular/Traditional Mode 1638 - 1950 Influenced but not defined by a particular style, vernacular buildings are made from easily available materials and exhibit local design characteristics. Example: 227 William Street, Page 14	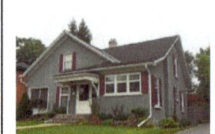
Victorian - In Ontario, a Victorian style building can be seen as any building built between 1840 and 1900 that doesn't fit into any of the other categories. It encompasses a large group of buildings constructed in brick, stone, and timber, using an eclectic mixture of Classical and Gothic motifs. Example: 191 Charles Street, Page 39	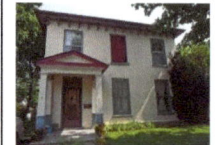

www.ingramcontent.com/pod-product-compliance
Lightning Source LLC
Chambersburg PA
CBHW040844180526
45159CB00001B/305